Speaking Up at Work

Speaking Up at Work

Leading Change as an Independent Thinker

Ryan E. Smerek

BUSINESS EXPERT PRESS

Leader in applied, concise business books

First published in 2023 by
Business Expert Press, LLC
222 East 46th Street, New York, NY 10017
www.businessexpertpress.com

ISBN-13: 978-1-63742-479-7 (paperback)
ISBN-13: 978-1-63742-480-3 (e-book)

Business Expert Press Human Resource Management and Organizational Behavior Collection

First edition: 2023

10 9 8 7 6 5 4 3 2 1

Description

If you have ever feared speaking up about your ideas or have done so but are frustrated by your lack of success, this book is for you.

You'll learn from the stories of others who have been a "lone voice" or an "independent thinker" and their attempts at change—both successful and unsuccessful. By learning from their experiences, you'll gain insight into effective tactics and pitfalls to avoid. In addition, if you are a leader and afraid you are not hearing the best ideas from your team, you'll learn various tools and tactics to let the best ideas emerge.

Along with stories ranging from CEOs to individual contributors, you'll learn insights from studies in psychology and management and what has been found through decades of research. Together the book offers an engaging portrait of when, why, and how to have your voice heard at work and in life.

Keywords

leading change; organizational change; innovation; employee voice; speaking up; speak-up culture; persuasion

Contents

Testimonials ix

Acknowledgments...xi

Chapter 1   Introduction 1

Chapter 2   Cultivating a Capacity for Independent Thinking 23

Chapter 3   Persuading Without Authority.........................53

Chapter 4   Leading Change 83

Chapter 5   Promoting Independent Thinking.................105

Chapter 6   Regretting Inaction and the Road Ahead 129

Notes..145

References 155

About the Author..167

Index 169

Testimonials

"An engaging, evidence-based, and actionable read about how to raise problems and solutions. From his extensive experience studying the challenges of speaking up, Ryan Smerek offers vivid examples and useful guidance to help you make sure your best ideas get the attention they deserve."—**Adam Grant, #1** *New York Times* **bestselling author of** *Think Again* **and host of the TED podcasts WorkLife and Re:Thinking**

"Ryan Smerek masterfully explores the difficult activities of speaking up and independent thinking by interweaving evidence from first-person interviews with relevant research and frameworks to produce accessible guidelines that lead to impactful original thinking. These ideas redescribe the quality of leadership in an important new way!"—**Karl E. Weick, Rensis Likert Distinguished University Professor of Organizational Behavior (Emeritus), University of Michigan**

"Self-censorship and self-editing are prevalent in our current organizations and in society. Being fearful of being ostracized, criticized, punished, or just offensive to others for articulating one's perspective is common. In this environment, Ryan's book is not only badly needed, but it is crafted in a way that is both practical and grounded in proven principles. Most importantly, Ryan uses the experiences of real people who have demonstrated how to navigate this territory effectively. You will learn a lot from Ryan's book on how to effectively exercise your voice."—**Kim Cameron, William Russell Kelly Professor Emeritus of Management and Organizations and Professor Emeritus of Higher Education, University of Michigan**

"In these times of uncertainty and competing definitions of any situation, it is more important than ever to become an independent thinker. This timely and well-written book shows you how to use critical thinking, truth

and reason, and evidence instead of fiction and opinion to have your voice heard and to lead positive change in your organization and your life."
—**Wayne E. Baker, Robert P. Thome Professor of Business Administration, University of Michigan Ross School of Business, and author of** ***All You Have to Do Is Ask***

Acknowledgments

This book would not have been possible without the openness and candidness of everyone who agreed to be interviewed, showing the importance you hold in research and discovery. Your stories were an inspiration to me and, given the constraints of confidentiality, I cannot thank you by name. I can thank, by name, Larry Bouts and Wendy Addison. Larry Bouts provided an impressive story of speaking up about innovative ideas and the constraints of most organizations. Wendy provided a painful but redemptive story of standing up against corruption. Thank you both.

For reviewing chapters of the manuscript and providing feedback, Kevin Schnieders, Dan Gruber, Chak Fu Lam, Eric Fridman, Curt Wang, and Eric Doctors. Thank you for your willingness to contribute to this work and for your thoughtful feedback. And Kevin Schnieders for being an inspirational servant leader and sharing how you create a positive culture where individuals can speak up.

To my parents, Ed and Cathy, for your support and encouragement with this project. And to Briana, for your editing, advice, and support all along the way. Thank you.

CHAPTER 1

Introduction

If you are an individual who fears speaking up about your ideas or have done so but are frustrated by your lack of success, I wrote this book for you. You'll learn from the stories of others who have been a "lone voice" or an "independent thinker" and their attempts at change—both successful and unsuccessful. By learning from their experiences, you'll gain insight into effective tactics and pitfalls to avoid. In addition, if you are a leader and afraid you are not hearing the best ideas from your team, you'll learn various tools and tactics to let the best ideas emerge. As we explore this terrain, let's begin with stories of speaking up as an "independent thinker," including seeing an emerging trend.

Independent Thinking

A few years following his time in the U.S. Navy and graduate school, Larry Bouts was in charge of a business planning unit at PepsiCo in the early 1980s. On Larry's staff was a newly minted MBA named Bill who had an insatiable curiosity about consumer trends. One day, Bill came to Larry with an analysis of what he thought was a fascinating new trend—a potential market in bottled water. At the time, as far as Larry could tell, there weren't any major corporations paying attention to this trend, as the market was still small. However, it wasn't clear why anyone would pay for bottled water when water was free from taps and fountains. Bill reasoned that consumers might value the convenience and portability of bottled water and that there were emerging concerns about the quality of water, especially in the public arena. Larry and his team saw that the initial growth rate in bottled water was steep and geographically dispersed, evidence of a real consumer trend.

In thinking through the idea, Larry thought PepsiCo could enter this market quickly. They had a network of bottlers and each one purified their water before making any product. There were also distribution agreements with retailers that could facilitate a national launch, and Pepsi had excellent marketing capabilities to brand and market a new product effectively.

With growing enthusiasm, Larry and his team developed an extensive presentation of the market, the consumer trends, and a recommended approach to the new product. The result? The meeting went badly from the start. As Larry recalls, it was clear senior management was hostile to the idea. One VP condescendingly announced, "We are a soft drink company!" And Larry responded, "We should be a beverage company because people don't drink Pepsi 24/7. They drink other things during the course of their day." Larry left the meeting despondent, thinking his credibility was damaged and that he might be fired.

Similar scenarios unfolded with iced tea and coffee. In each scenario, Larry and his team's ideas were rejected. In recalling the potential to buy a large coffee distribution company in the mid-1980s, Larry recalled the CEO responding to him, "You don't understand, you idiot. We're in the soft drink business and coffee is a dead duck. It's a dying brand, dying idea. Nobody likes coffee anymore." When asked what made him receptive to these ideas in comparison to others, Larry says, "We believed the title that we were given, which was to build and expand the power of PepsiCo brands. In fact, our job more likely was to do what we were told." While the decisions by senior management at PepsiCo were short-sighted and obviously flawed in retrospect, Larry is still sympathetic to the position of executives. As he states:

> In defense of the company you can look at it another way. That is, the senior executives there were employed and paid richly to advance the company's products. If they would divert their attention into coffee, or into some other thing, and for some reason we'd lose a tenth of a market share, or 2/10ths of a market share on brand Pepsi, the bottlers would be outraged and would be up in arms. Senior exec's heads can roll over small losses in market share. And their view, and I can't say that they were wrong in the short term, is that every living moment, every living thing has to go towards maximizing the sale of the products that we have. The fact is though that short term maximization can lead to long term loss of relevance in any company.

Larry is describing a universal phenomenon of exploiting current products at the expense of exploring new ideas.[1] In a world of trade-offs and opportunity costs, it can be difficult to take our hand off the steering wheel and explore a new path, even for a short amount of time. As Larry experienced, with status quo bias and short-term performance pressures, it can be difficult to advocate exploring new avenues and opportunities.

Nevertheless, as we think about developing new ideas, we need to have an open mind, within limits, about what might be true. Part of having an open mind is trying to see reality and new evidence as objectively as possible, despite all the pressures one is facing. As Larry says,

> I think there's a lot of people who like to think differently. I think we see reality...We don't see things as we want them to be. We kind of try to see things as they are and are more fact-based.

This was partly the result of Larry's naval training, where accurately perceiving an external environment is essential. What you hope is happening in the conditions of combat or the weather is irrelevant to what is actually occurring. You can, of course, partly shape the world given your actions, as PepsiCo could have done in building demand for a new product, but, by and large, an accurate understanding of an external environment—free of willful distortions—helps us adapt and thrive for the future. Nevertheless, the world is evolving and despite clarity in retrospect, things are never so certain in the moment. This heightens the need for us to speak up at work and to promote independent thinking in our teams and organizations.

This book will explore the individual characteristics and situational conditions that lead an individual to develop an independent point of view and to openly voice this view regarding an organizational performance issue. The implications are to better understand how to encourage independent thinking and to understand the personality characteristics and developmental experiences that foster this ability.

In order to understand the experience of independent thinking in the workplace, I conducted over 50 interviews with individuals about numerous "voice events" throughout their working lives. Together, these individuals shared over 90 experiences.[2] The insights and stories from these individuals form one basis for the ideas in this book. Research in the field of management and psychology form the second.

But first, what is independent thinking? Independent thinking is working to make sense of the world to develop a well-reasoned point of view; it is not passively accepting dogma, authority, or tradition, and it is in service of improving the performance of the organization or upholding an important value.[3] We can see this in the case of Larry Bouts at PepsiCo. His team was actively seeking ways to improve the organization's long-term performance by discovering consumer trends.

To be an independent thinker, we have to perceive the world differently than everyone else. In an organizational context, when we perceive the world differently, it is often because of our prior experiences. While that may seem like a banal point, having experiences in multiple contexts allows us to bring the norms and ways of operating from those prior contexts into our current situation.

Take, for example, Tom.[4] Tom was a senior HR officer of a large technology company and the senior leaders of the firm were considering removing performance ratings for employees. The current performance management process was cumbersome, and to many employees, it was demeaning to have their performance for a year distilled to a single number. However, in opposition to his colleagues around the table, Tom thought performance ratings were a necessary means of differentiating performance and that getting rid of the numerical rating would only be treating a "symptom" and not the cause. The cause, in Tom's view, was the inability of managers to have meaningful conversations about performance. To Tom, the problem was managers not being trained to give meaningful, ongoing feedback, and his perspective on the topic was developed from his early "formative years" at a prior company. From his early experiences, he viewed these conversations as a learnable skill. Thus, Tom's ability to think independently was a result of his formative years in another context, and this experience led him to be the main voice of dissent in his current situation.

Given Tom's dissent at a senior executive meeting that they *should* keep performance ratings, they split into two teams: the ratings team and the no-ratings team. Tom was the head of the "ratings team," and they visited several companies to understand their performance management practices. Nevertheless, Tom felt that he was "swimming upstream" by wanting to keep the ratings "because of a combination of a management feeling, 'Hey look this is too hard to do, let's rip the Band-Aid off.' Also, the literature was red hot with this." Tom didn't feel threatened as he spearheaded the opposing point of view. He was head of talent for the company and "had the platform to be able to do this and say this." Tom mentions he wasn't contentious in how he stated his viewpoint but was clear that he thought the company would be "addressing a symptom, not the problem."

In the end, Tom lost the battle when ratings were, in fact, removed from the performance evaluation process. Nevertheless, Tom's ability to perceive the situation differently was a result of his formative years in another organization. He saw things differently and how the organization could operate more effectively. While his point of view did not ultimately prevail, his dissent helped improve the quality of the decision-making process. It did this by sparking a "healthy dialog" that "energized the organization" and helped with implementation. As Tom states, "imagine if we had just imposed this without going through the exercise of dialog." This process helped anticipate issues of removing ratings and addressed potential concerns. Of course, this process was less efficient than a quick decision, but Tom mentions, in addition to helping with implementation, the process allowed him to advocate for "more thoughtful goal setting" and "more robust and specific feedback." Thus, the process of dissent—as uncomfortable as it can be individually—helped improve the implementation of the decision.

Because Tom spoke up with a point of view based on his prior experience, you might argue that there is no such thing as independent thinking, that all thinking is social. As Alan Jacobs argues in his book *How to Think*, "To think independently of other human beings is impossible, and if it were possible it would be undesirable. Thinking is necessarily, thoroughly, and wonderfully social."[5] It's true that we think through ideas with others, but in the sense that I am using the term independent thinking, it is about articulating an independent point of view with respect to your group. Although your point of view may have been formed within another social group many years ago, at present you are an independent voice, with perhaps some known support. To say that all thinking is social comes close to a truism, as it overstates the case that in many circumstances we will think through a point of view independently, without direct conversation with others.[6] We may be relying on ideas we've read, conversations long past, or building upon a prior work experience, but in the moment, we are an independent voice.

To more precisely see the experience of being an independent voice, let's examine one of the seminal studies in social psychology. The topics of independence and conformity have been central to social psychology since the 1950s and one of the foundational studies can give us clues about the prevalence and experience of independent thinking.

Believing Your Own Eyes

Imagine yourself sitting around a table with eight other individuals. You are all shown two cards; the first card has a line that is six inches long and the second card has three separate lines (Figure 1.1). One of the lines on this second card is also six inches long and the other two lines are noticeably longer or shorter. Your task is fairly simple: name which line on the second card (A, B, or C) is the same length as the line on the first card.[7]

Unbeknownst to you, the other eight individuals are actors who will each give the same wrong answer. You are seated next to last and have to state your judgment after unanimous responses before you that are incorrect compared to what you see. What would you do? Do you think there must be something wrong with your eyes? Do you give in to doubt that you must be misguided? Or, do you nevertheless state what you plainly see is true?

Card One   Card Two

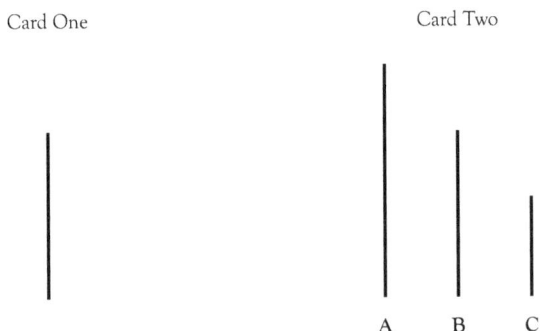

Figure 1.1 Asch line judgment task

This was the experiment that Solomon Asch ran in the 1950s, in which participants completed 18 such line judgment trials. For each participant, on 12 of the 18 instances, called "critical trials," the actors all give the same wrong answer. Solomon Asch found that out of the 123 individuals that went through this experiment, 29 people (24 percent) always spoke what they knew to be true. For every time they were asked which line was identical to the others, they gave the correct answer, despite everyone prior to them saying another answer. Only 6 people, out of the 123 (5 percent), conformed with the group on all 12 critical trials. The rest varied along a continuum, with some conforming all the time and some never conforming. Across all critical trials and participants, individuals gave a correct judgment 63 percent of the time. This is either wonderful or horrid, depending on your perspective. The situation *was* powerful, but 63 percent of the time, a person gave a correct judgment in the face of clear unanimity. To be clear, the length of lines was not ambiguous, such that if you squinted, reasonable people might disagree. It was clear which line matched the others as demonstrated by a control group who reviewed the materials and made a mistake in only 1 percent of cases.

In follow-up interviews that Asch conducted, there were a wide variety of responses about the experience, with some of the individuals doubting their perceptual faculties (i.e., something must be wrong with me). As several participants stated, "Maybe my eyes were going bad." "My whole mental processes were working abnormally."[8] As Asch states, those who remained independent were not free from doubt, but they were able to "free themselves of it."[9] Asch also found discomfort among individuals with being at the center of attention. As one individual who remained completely independent stated, "You have the idea that the attention of the group is focused on you."[10] There was also an oppressive sense of loneliness in being separate from the group. As Asch summarizes:

> Many stressed the sense of loneliness at being separated from others. This feeling merged with an oppressive sense of the contrast between the apparently supreme security of the majority and their own bewilderment: "So many against me—so many sure of one thing."[11]

Asch also found that among participants who yielded, they nearly always underestimated the degree to which they did so, often guessing only a few times when in fact it was closer to seven or eight instances. Along with an underestimation of one's yielding was a disappointment at doing so. One participant who yielded only once on the 12 conformity trials replied, "If I only hadn't chickened out, it would have been an even dozen." He then continued:

> I think my father would be very sore at me for that one I missed. He would expect me to always do what I know or think is right because it is right. My mother too. Don't know why I fooled myself into thinking there might be some doubt about it.[12]

Here, we see an individual who let himself down and who communicates a sense of dismay at having "fooled" himself.

Among individuals who readily conformed, Asch found participants whose meaning system was wholly comprised of conforming to expectations. This is what Robert Kegan, an adult developmental psychologist, calls having a "socialized mind."[13] A socialized mind doesn't yet have an independent seat of judgment and is primarily concerned with living out the dictates of others. At the extreme, you might think of individuals who are "good soldiers"; they don't question orders, not even internally to themselves. As one participant states,

> Am wondering now...what they think of me for following... I went with them, not only because I was sure I was wrong and didn't want to be the only one disagreeing, but because I was sure I was wrong and didn't want to foul up your statistics.[14]

From this participant, we can see the ready acceptance of the majority's judgment as correct, along with a concern for dutifully complying with the perceived expectations of the experimenter. No thought is given to the accuracy of one's perceptions, but rather the meaning system of the individual is wholly comprised of conforming to others.

Among individuals who remained independent, Asch interpreted the ability to do so with a secure sense of "personal worth."[15] Individuals felt confident in themselves to deviate from the group. Their self-worth was not immediately contingent upon the group's acceptance. Our sense of personal worth derives from many sources, which includes our job security and status in the organization. In the stories we've already seen, Larry Bouts had been approached with other job opportunities so he wasn't afraid to think independently about the future strategy of the organization. In the case of Tom, he had status among his peers as the head of talent. Thus, one facilitator of independence is a secure sense of personal worth derived from a variety of sources, including our network of supportive relationship, job opportunities, status, and being a member of a dominant identity group. We'll look at several of these factors, along with personality dispositions that foster independence, in Chapter 2.

So what does Asch's study teach us about the prevalence of independent thinking? Based on Asch's study, we can hypothesize a baseline of 25 percent of individuals remaining completely independent, partly based on a secure sense of personal worth. I think we can safely say that 25 percent is the upper limit of what we might expect in organizations. In the psychology experiment, by disagreeing with the group, none of the individuals faced the prospect of losing their job, losing a future promotion, or retribution on a performance review. They faced a one-shot experience with a group of strangers. In addition, this issue was a matter of black-and-white, not an issue fraught with ambiguity, nor a prediction of how an uncertain future will unfold (e.g., "I don't think this strategy will work"). In the more ambiguous cases we face every day, it seems more likely we'll give into doubts and assume the majority must know something we do not. In contrast, whether the length of a line matches the length of another is not of great personal importance. While it might be disorienting and have you questioning your perceptual abilities, it isn't likely to upset your moral sensibilities, which would increase your likelihood of dissent. Thus, while an exact number is contingent upon situational conditions, it's likely that the percentage of individuals who remain independent is somewhere below 25 percent.

In the Asch study (and in everyday life), there are two main forms of social influence—informational and normative. Informational social influence is the belief that "everyone else can't be wrong, they must know something that I don't." Normative social influence is the desire to belong and be accepted by the group.[16] As you can imagine, the more ambiguous and complex an issue becomes, the likelihood of informational social influence increases. Given we perceive others to have more expertise than us, we're likely to assume they know something we do not. With normative social influence, our point of view is motivated by wanting social acceptance.

More recently, as fMRI machines have been added to the toolkit of scientists, researchers have examined what occurs in the brain when remaining independent.[17] In one experiment while in an fMRI machine, participants saw two cubed-objects and had to determine whether the two objects were identical, but just rotated images. By "cubed-objects," imagine an object created from approximately 10 Lego squares with one or two right-angles and branches. Next to that image, there is a rotated image that may or may not be identical. You have to mentally rotate the first image in your head to "see" if the two are identical. As with the Asch experiments, this creates a judgment with a nonambiguous standard of correctness. In this experiment, three seconds before you see the two objects, you see four small pictures of fellow participants and their judgment of whether the rotated images are the same or different. As you'd expect, the other people were confederates and their responses were predetermined. There were 48 trials and sometimes the group was unanimously correct and sometimes the group was unanimously incorrect. In addition, there were a few "split decisions" by confederates to increase the believability of the task.

One question this experiment helps answer is whether conformity happens at the level of perception. Because participants see the group's judgment in advance, when the group's judgment is incorrect, do participants perceive the world likewise? Or do they consciously deliberate and decide to conform? If conformity happens at the level of perception with no deliberation, the road to independence is much more difficult. We do not even *perceive* a conflict. The group's judgment immediately becomes our own. If we do consciously deliberate, we have more of an opening to promote independence.

First, the researchers found that there was substantial conformity based on the confederates' answers. Respondents were three times as likely to give the wrong answer when the group was unanimously incor-rect.[18] Next, the researchers found that when subjects wrongly conformed to the group, there was activity in the perceptual regions of the brain, not in the frontal areas of the cortex, which occurs if there is conscious deliberation. This supports the notion that conformity is happening at the level of *perception*, not deliberation. We see what others think and don't make the effort to figure out an answer for ourselves. This is partly the result of the *efficiency principle* of the brain.[19] It's more efficient to go with the herd and not waste our cognitive resources. From a cognitive perspective, this is one reason for the prevalence of conformity. We both perceive the world in accordance with others and do not want to engage in the effort to think through a point of view for ourselves. Nevertheless, in the experiment *itself*, many individuals did think independently and provided a different answer than the group—countering an understand-able tendency to preserve one's cognitive resources. In the cases where individuals were independent, there was greater activation of the right amygdala, which the researchers conclude is the "pain of independence." Whether it was painful or not, the amygdala activation explains the emo-tional arousal instigated by independence. This corroborates numerous examples throughout this book where individuals discuss their dislike of being a "lone voice."

Take, for example, Cheryl's experience of being a dissenting mem-ber of a private board. Cheryl was halfway through a three-year term on a 22-member board of a private school and became the "lone voice of dissension" to approve a capital campaign to build a new building. The headmaster wanted to start a capital campaign for a $30 million build-ing, which could include a substantial amount of debt. In explaining her decision to dissent, Cheryl states:

> We were in the board meeting and I was just—we were caught by surprise…The head of school had an ally who basically said, "Let's vote today," and it just caught everybody off guard. And catching people off guard is a very strategic move and a very calculated move. And I just—I realized in that moment, no one else was going to speak up…I just raised my hand and I said, "I couldn't vote today."

The capital campaign was to be five times the size of anything the school had previously undertaken, and to Cheryl's mind,

> just looking at it and having seen the financial models, they hadn't modeled out how to—how to bridge a gap between what we had raised in the past and what they were trying to raise in the future to build a building…We had a fairly good understanding from development that we could probably raise about 12 million of the 30 million that was being proposed. And the concern was, well, if we only raised 12 million, what are we going to do?

This meant potential debt financing and tuition increases that could "change the mission of the school." As Cheryl says:

> I couldn't reconcile not vocalizing my discomfort with the actions that the board was taking. We were getting down to a kind of a watershed vote…on launching a substantial capital campaign for the school. And I just—I felt like we didn't have enough information…to vote and that we were potentially putting the company—the school's long-term financial situation at risk… and so, because of that I just felt like I just ethically couldn't go forward without taking a stand.

Even though Cheryl wouldn't lose her livelihood by being a dissenting vote, her "heart raced" in taking this position. As a board member, Cheryl was in a privileged position. Nevertheless, the emotional cost and courage it took to dissent was high. If this had been Cheryl's full-time job, the pressure to conform would have been even higher. As it was, Cheryl and her husband had a child in the school, a factor that led another board member to stay silent for fear of "ticking off the headmaster." Regardless, as Cheryl recalls,

> it was very uncomfortable because it was just not who I am typically. After the meeting, I received some phone calls from board directors who were really kind of ticked. And said, you know, "It must feel very lonely to be the lone voice of dissension."

What strengthened Cheryl was she knew she wasn't the only person who thought additional planning needed to take place, but she was the only person "vocalizing dissent." As she remarks, "I wasn't the lone dissenter. I was the lone voice of dissension." Having an ally, whether that person is silent or not, is critical to withstanding the social force of conformity, as found in numerous studies.[20] As Cheryl mentions, "I had a level of bravery because I knew I wasn't alone. I don't know if I was completely alone if I would have done it if I'm being really honest." Having an ally was small comfort, however, given the experience she faced, but it helped her take a stand, given she knew there were others who supported her view privately but who did not want to speak up.

Given her dissent, the board dispersed, and they had weekly executive committee meetings before the next board meeting in a month. The elapsed time "opened the door" for people to say, "Hey, I have some questions." Organizationally, this is a positive outcome of dissent because by breaking conformity, it "opens the door" for other people to ask questions, thus improving a group's deliberation and decision making. The board chairman called every board member individually to see what they would need to vote. By the next meeting, the board ended up creating safeguards by needing to raise 80 percent of the capital before groundbreaking. They also agreed that they wouldn't do any long-term debt financing that would lead to tuition increases.[21]

Through the experience, Cheryl says she's

learned that I can share my thoughts through questions rather than through opinions and that rather than saying, "I disagree," I can say, "Should we consider? What happens if? You know, can we?" And that it's likely to be met with less resistance than [saying] "I completely disagree and here's why.'

While Cheryl was effective in helping the school avoid financial difficulties, it was an arduous victory, and she did not serve another three-year term, despite being asked to. As she says,

Part of the reason that I decided not to take the second term is I actually did not feel good being a positive deviant. I did not like it at all. I felt sick. It was a horrible experience. I did not enjoy it. I do not enjoy being in the center of conflict.

In Cheryl's story, we can see the emotional turmoil of the experience of dissent, of going against the will of the majority and feeling shunned. Why bother? Why go through the emotional difficulty? It's a fair point and takes us to strategically "picking your battles" and knowing your personal comfort with conflict. Cheryl mentions she does not revel in conflict. Some people do. The task of dissent for them is an easier haul. In Cheryl's case, this was an important issue for her. Had the school fallen into financial disarray, she thought the likelihood of tuition increases would make the school too expensive for low-income families. If this did occur, she'd experience regret at her prior inaction. This is an underappreciated driver of action—imagined regret. We do things in the present to avoid regret in the future. We shield ourselves—as best we can—from future distress by speaking up in the moment. This is the meaning of the oft-used phrase, "I wouldn't be able to live with myself." In these cases, it's not that we are calculating future probabilities and taking action based on these tabulations. In fact, it's unlikely Cheryl went through any calculus in the exact moment of dissent. She was compelled in the moment and was suspicious of the rushed vote. Her dissent was both intuitively compelled and reasoned—spurring action and helping the group make a better decision.

Cheryl's story is also a real-life analog to the Asch line-judgment conformity experiment. Everyone went along, but Cheryl was the lone voice of dissent. Similar to the Asch participants (and the modern-day fMRI version), we can see the emotional turmoil in dissenting, but with psychology studies, we have a nonambiguous standard of correctness. We know individuals were correct when they deviated from the group. For Cheryl, however, was she correct in dissenting? The situation is difficult because Cheryl couldn't point to a recognizable standard of correctness. She was dissenting about financial assumptions that were predictions of the future—something no one can be certain of. Furthermore, she was partially motivated by her value-based judgment that *if* the school could not raise enough money, *then* they would have to raise tuition, which *might* make the school too expensive for low-income families. Again, even if this were to occur, the value of wanting to make the education of the school affordable to low-income families may not be shared by other board members. All of this points to the difficulty of dissent without recourse to concrete facts, which brings us to the fact–value distinction.

Fact–Value Distinction

Psychology experiments are helpful because they have a nonambiguous standard of correctness. We are judging black-and-white facts, not taking a stand based on an important value. As we've already seen, there is a distinction between whether an individual is taking a stand based on facts or a value—and an implied prediction if this value is disregarded. As with the story of Larry Bouts, he and his team came to see bottled water as an emerging trend. His advocacy and viewpoint were based on an empirically verifiable external environment and a prediction based on this evidence. It was not a stand he took because he valued the health benefits of drinking water over soft drinks. It was based on evidence of an emerging trend.

In contrast, many respondents discussed taking a stand based on an important value, similar to Cheryl's concern for tuition becoming too high for low-income families. For example, one respondent discussed taking a stand at a meeting when he thought the department head was unfairly criticizing a colleague as a low-performing teacher. In this case, the motivation to take a stand was not compelled by analysis of what was objectively true, but rather the value of how an individual should be treated, and in this case, he believed the organization held more responsibility to effectively train the teacher rather than to shame the person for low performance. While this case involves a values-based response of how people should be treated, it still implies how the future will unfold if this value is ignored. For example, other people will be demoralized and leave the organization, or if we treat people better, our performance will improve.

But what are values exactly? Values are an umbrella term that refer to "trans-situational goals, varying in importance, that serve as guiding principles in the life of a person or group."[22] They are affectively laden, which gives them a positive or negative valence, and the emotions they evoke—when beyond a threshold—compel action.[23] The definition of values also highlights that they vary in importance. As individuals, we develop a hierarchy of values that is mostly implicit. We may value treating others with kindness and respect more than we value obedience to authority, for example. Given we have this implicit hierarchy, one can quickly see how it can, in certain situations, become a source of conflict.

In thinking through the difference between facts and values, we can see the difference by articulating cases that clearly fall in either category. However, the difference can become quite blurry. What facts we perceive can be value-laden. Nevertheless, we do not want to discard the notion that there are facts and an objective reality that is occurring and we want to see this as clearly as possible. In the case of bottled water, for example, you wouldn't want to take a "subjectivist stance" toward its emergence (e.g., "Susan thinks bottled water will be a large trend in the future, but Bob thinks it won't. I guess we all have our different points-of-view"). Rather, we want to take a rationalist stance toward knowledge, meaning "despite the uncertainty of knowledge, some beliefs—those with stronger evidence—should be considered more certain than others."[24]

Many of the incidents we'll see involve a value-based argument about the future performance of the organization. What was challenging in most of these cases is that there was not a recognizable standard to prove one's position in the moment. For example, the ability to gain facts and evidence in support of your position is limited when you are an independent voice against a majority in a hiring decision. You can argue from facts of the applicant's background, but your prediction of the person's future performance is often value-laden, about the type of person that should be hired and the value that should be placed on their relative strengths and weaknesses. In other cases, there is a more recognizable standard of correctness. In the investment world, for example, there is agreement that the eventual standard of correctness is the rate of return on an investment asset. There is more clarity on the goal that is being pursued, and arguments can be directly made with respect to that goal. And, in the future, you can know with less ambiguity whether your judgments were correct or not.

When we have disagreements at work, it is often over how a future will unfold. We have different value-based predictions about what might happen. However, when that future does arrive, the counterfactual of a different path is unknown. We do not know if we were "correct" because our candidate was not hired or our strategy was not implemented. We do not have a counterfactual world that unfolded to comparatively analyze. Occasionally, there may be unambiguous cases where an employee you argued against was still offered a position and you are proven correct by some fatal flaw that is revealed. Or, as was explained with Larry Bouts and advocating for bottled water, the future does unequivocally unfold as predicted. Thus, situations vary to the extent that they are fact-based or value-based and how hard it is to know the correctness of any judgment in the moment. Figure 1.2 outlines these two coexisting domains. The important point is even if we are advocating a belief, prediction, or judgment and we know that correctness is elusive, we do not move toward pure relativism (i.e., everyone has their different perspectives), but try as best we can to take an "evaluativist" position, where we ground our judgments and beliefs in reasons, facts, and evidence as best we can.[25]

So, if a recognizable standard of correctness is elusive, how are most decisions made? Researchers of social influence mention that when no shared criteria for a correct solution exist, the size and authority of the faction favoring an alternative usually wins.[26] In organizations, while the size of a faction can be influential, the authority structure (i.e., who is in charge) often makes the final decision. The most interesting cases, however, are when a minority faction (or lone voice) is able

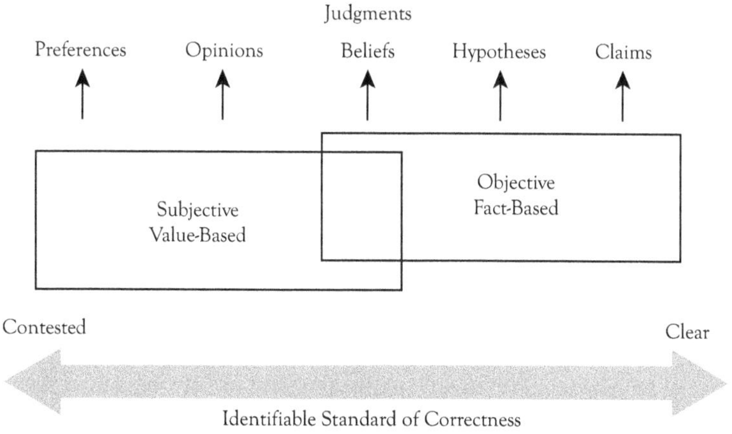

Figure 1.2 Fact–value continuum

to persuade a majority even without authority. These cases are rare and often require a great deal of consistency and conviction over time. It requires being persuasive and getting others to think differently. For even if we are in a factual domain with a verifiable standard of correctness (e.g., financial investments), the scenario of plainly outlining facts that convince every stakeholder is implausible without resounding evidence, which rarely exists.

All of this is to say that a standard of correctness is often elusive, independence is often a result of conflicting values that cannot be *proven* per se, and feedback cycles of correctness are often long or nonexistent. None of this means we should abandon reasoning from facts and evidence where possible. And, although we may be a lone minority in the moment, there are, of course, many instances where a majority is slowly persuaded by a minority opinion based on the conviction and reasoning of that minority. Even if the majority is not persuaded in the moment, we'll look at the motivation and willingness to try, even if it feels like we are "shouting at the wind."

Model of Independent Thinking

Figure 1.3 is a model that helps frame this book. At the center of independent thinking is the motivation to improve the organization, prevent a negative outcome, or a value-based stance that has evoked an emotional response. The three of these intermix, as a desire to *improve* the organization is often the result of helping the group *avoid* a negative future outcome, but they can be distinguished. A desire to improve the organization is often making suggestions that might advance the performance trajectory of the group beyond the steady state. It is a suggestion that is often discretionary and a new direction the organization might pursue— much like investing in bottled water. In contrast, the desire to prevent a negative outcome may be voicing an issue that has the potential to ruin the organization if not dealt with. In the field of employee voice, the desire to improve the organization is called *promotive voice* whereas the desire to help avoid a negative outcome is called *prohibitive voice*.[27] Again, while these two can be distinguished, in many respects they are two sides of the same coin.

In addition, I distinguish a third motive which is a values-based response. This could also be concerned with promoting positive outcomes or prohibiting negative ones, but it is derived more from an individual's sense of right and wrong. The decision to speak up might help the organization improve, but it is primarily driven by a sense of injustice and anger, such as the forced ranking of employees or the harmful treatment of a low-performing employee. These three motives—a desire to improve or to prevent a negative outcome and a values-based response—can be distinguished by clear cases that illustrate each motive as foreground, with the other motives involved but working as background.

All of this leads to an evaluation of whether speaking up will be efficacious or futile and the cost/benefits of doing so. Given there is time to deliberate, an individual decides whether speaking up will make any difference, and, if in doing so, the benefits will outweigh the costs. There are real costs for sharing one's point of view, including future retaliation and being dismissed and disliked for being a deviant. In contrast, however, offering an independent point of view that leads to real improvement can accrue benefits to one's career. We'll see some of these positive examples in the stories ahead.

Although there is often deliberation about efficacy and cost/benefits, in some situations, this deliberation may be bypassed. You instantaneously speak up and dissent—the perceived "rightness" of your position drives you to take a stance. In these situations, the perceived futility of dissent is subsumed under acting with integrity: "It's just the right thing to do," a person might say, or "I would not be able to sleep at night." These are matters of personal conscience where deliberation about cost and benefits are secondary, if they occur at all.

As you might imagine, the outcomes of speaking up are manifold. In the best scenarios, improvements are made, and with this the individual has a greater sense of efficacy, commitment, and perception of fairness. At the very least, by speaking up the group may reconsider and further refine its approach, as we saw with Tom arguing that the organization should keep its performance ratings. In the worst scenarios, an individual is ostracized, retaliated against, and openly or secretly despised. On balance—while every situation has its risks—the benefits of independent thinking, as I'll argue throughout this book, often outweigh the costs.

Leadership Facilitators:

- Engage in democratic over autocratic leadership
- Be actively open-minded
- Promote the expectation to speak up
- Foster norm to ask "Is it true?"
- Facilitate group ideation sessions
- Directly solicit ideas
- Facilitate healthy debate w/ alternative viewpoints

Persuasiveness:

- Appropriately regulate emotions (e.g., anger)
- Ask questions vs. being direct
- Effectively present evidence
- Choose message medium
- Procedural considerations with stakeholders
- Utilize social proof
- Build credibility and align issue w/ org. values

Outcomes:

- Decision-making (+)
- Innovative improvements (+)
- Individual career outcomes (+/−)
- Individual motivation and satisfaction (+/−)

Speaking up process

Situational Evaluation:

- Perceived efficacy or futility of voice
- Perceived cost/benefits of voice
- Perceived "rightness" of position

Leading Change:

- Engage in discovery
- Create dissatisfaction with status quo
- Adopt an experimental mindset
- Use comprehensive tactics for voluntary change
- Avoid "reactance" by promoting involvement
- Take a calculated risk to prove idea

Motivation:

- Desire to improve the organization
- Desire to prevent negative future outcomes
- Values-based response (e.g., moral emotion)

Individual Facilitators:

- Be a critical thinker/build expertise
- Utilize an "outsider perspective"
- Be curious/follow hunches
- Establish a sense of self-worth
- Value reason and truth
- Behave with integrity to professional norms

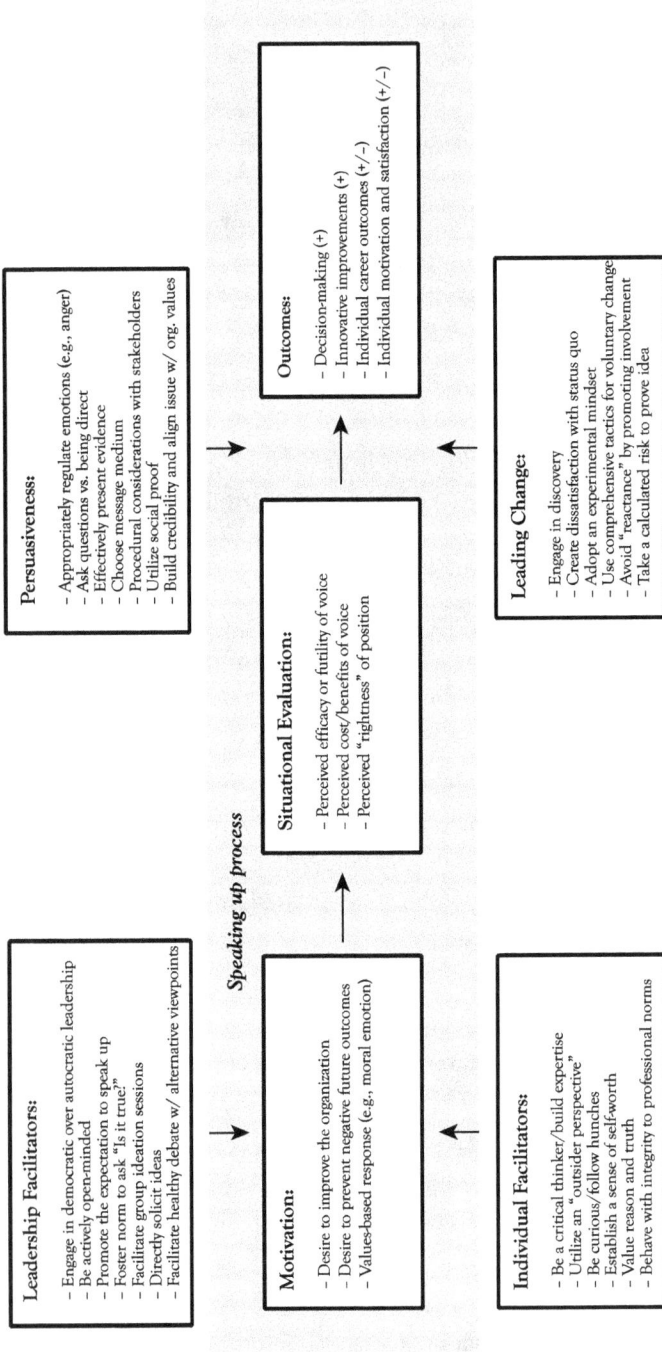

Figure 1.3 Model for understanding independent thinking

Around this brief sketch of speaking up are the facilitators of doing so. We'll first explore ways to cultivate a capacity for independent thinking, including (1) critical thinking and domain expertise, (2) being an outsider, (3) curiosity and a willingness to follow "slow hunches," (4) a secure sense of "personal worth" that allows you to face the vulnerability of looking "stupid," (5) the value placed on reason and truth, and (6) behaving with a sense of professional integrity.

As an individual without formal authority, if you believe it's worth speaking up, the likelihood of change occurring also depends on the persuasiveness of your message. I'll cover the numerous ways in which your message can be more persuasive, including regulating your emotions (e.g., anger), using social proof from external groups, and trying to slowly persuade through questions (e.g., What do you think of…?) versus being more direct and forceful.

After exploring the *how* of speaking up, I'll broaden the scope to explore the process of leading change when you have minimal authority. We'll look at what you should do next if you get a green light on your idea. What are effective strategies in leading change? And if you don't get a green light, in some circumstances, do you proceed anyway?

We'll then look at specific leadership facilitators that can promote greater employee voice, including a leadership style that is more democratic than autocratic, setting the expectation for "getting at the truth," and specific tactics to overcome groupthink.

As we explore different components of this framework, let's start with better understanding the individual factors that promote independent thinking.

CHAPTER 2

Cultivating a Capacity for Independent Thinking

At the individual level, what are some of the dispositions that help support independent thinking? Is it something you are *born* with or can you cultivate a capacity to think independently? We'll explore these questions throughout this chapter. Let's start with a paragon of independent thinking in the investment world.

Critical Thinking and Being an Outsider

To understand independent thinking, one exemplar from the investment world is Michael Burry.[1] Burry made hundreds of millions in the financial crisis of 2008 by seeing that the housing market was overheated and that many banks were mortally exposed to the risk of homeowners defaulting on their mortgages. However, this was barely seen by most investors, bankers, and policy makers (as well as the American public at large). What led Burry to be able to see what others couldn't see?

As author Micheal Lewis recounts, when Burry was at age two, he had cancer near his left eye, leaving him with a glass eye. This led Burry to see himself as different, and this, along with a general social awkwardness, made it difficult for Burry to make friends. He would remain an outsider in most social situations. As Burry states, "My natural state is an outsider, and no matter what group I'm in or where I am, I always felt like I'm outside the group, and I've always been analyzing the group."[2]

Before entering the world of investments, Burry tried a career in medicine. After finishing medical school in 1998, Burry moved to Stanford University for a neurology residency. In the late evenings, he would spend his time studying financial documents to make investments, and it soon became evident that medicine wasn't his true passion. Thus, Burry decided to quit his residency in 2000 and begin investing full time. He would use a small amount of money from family and an even larger amount from investors that had read an investment blog he was writing during the evenings of his medical residency. That several prominent investors would give him money, solely based on the analysis of his investment blog, is remarkable in itself. It indicates the insight of his analysis and the ability to see things differently.

In the early 2000s, as Burry studied various markets, he would begin to see what many others did not see, that lending standards in the housing market had deteriorated to such a degree that individuals were being given interest-only mortgages where no principal was being paid. In addition, interest rates on many of these mortgages were set to spike many years after low "teaser rates." While we can see the housing bubble in retrospect, at the time, government leaders and financial institutions had limited or no sense of the systemic risk to the economy. As Burry recounts in a presentation he gave in 2011:

> Amidst early fears that the housing market was getting ahead of itself in 2003, Fed Chairman Alan Greenspan assured everyone that national bubbles in real estate simply do not happen. As I surveyed the national trends in housing at that time, I wondered whether common sense ought rule against the application of precedent to the unprecedented.[3]

Burry saw very clearly a disconnect in lending. Over several decades, banks were becoming less concerned whether borrowers were creditworthy because they would bundle the loans into mortgage-backed securities and sell them to Wall Street. The bundling left an individual loan officer at a bank unconcerned whether a borrower could repay the loan—as they historically were—because they would receive the commission on the sale of a mortgage-backed security regardless. Furthermore, it was argued that by diversifying mortgages into larger pools, risk was minimized. It was presumed that while one individual might default on their mortgage, there wouldn't be systemic defaults based on a large-scale housing bubble. That was the consensus Michael Burry would question.

Given his independent perspective, there was no vehicle for Burry to bet that a mortgage-backed security would falter. He had to get Wall Street to create a credit default swap on these securities, and few banks had any interest in dealing with him. As Lewis recounts,

> when Michael Burry pestered firms in the beginning of 2005, only Deutsche Bank and Goldman Sachs had any real interest in continuing the conversation. No one on Wall Street, as far as he could tell, saw what he was seeing.[4]

Remarkably, Burry avoided Bear Stearns and Lehman Brothers—both firms that would collapse in the financial crisis in 2008—because he states, "I viewed both to be mortally exposed to the crisis I foresaw."[5]

Although Burry's story is slightly different from others in this book in that he was the head of a small investment firm and didn't face the conformity pressures of most employees, he still faced constant pressure and skepticism from his investors. It wasn't an easy journey, as investors were constantly concerned that he had moved away from his strategy of picking individual companies that were undervalued, to trying to predict macroeconomic trends—an endeavor that is more precarious.[6] As Burry recounts, "I almost think the better the idea, and the more iconoclastic the investor, the more likely you will get screamed at by investors."[7] Nevertheless, Burry would persevere through difficult times with his investors, including "side-pocketing" their money which made it unavailable for them to withdraw. In the end, his analysis paid off. At the end of 2007, he would realize profits of $720 million, on a portfolio of less than $550 million.[8]

A skeptic might argue that there is no real lesson in Michael Burry's story. With hundreds of thousands of investors prodding every loophole, some are bound to be right at certain times—a broken clock is right twice a day. It's true that we risk oversimplifying by only recounting success stories. We don't recount the thousands of cases where people had an independent point of view but were wrong. Perhaps they have the same profile as Michael Burry. Burry was just lucky, and not skilled, as some might argue. As Alan Greenspan, former chairman of the Federal Reserve, argued, Burry just had "beginner's luck" and that his returns were a "statistical illusion."[9] I think this is too dismissive and gives no credence to reason, logic, and perceptual clarity. It is true, as a manager of investments, Burry didn't face the conformity pressures as intense at most companies. He was an outsider to Wall Street and not beholden to the mainstream consensus. However, his story illustrates the importance of taking an "outsider perspective," either embodied in an individual who is an "outsider" or as a perspective we try to take ourselves.

Burry's story also illustrates independent thinking that is more than a passing opinion. He didn't have a vague notion that it seemed like lending standards had deteriorated. He did complex calculations and *actually* read the prospectuses of mortgage-backed securities to make hundred million-dollar bets. His analysis was far from the consensus and was proven correct. It was proven correct in trades against Wall Street firms who had very talented individuals and leaders of investment banks who had every reason to see the risk their firms were taking. This is most striking for Bear Stearns and Lehman Brothers, who collapsed under their exposure to mortgage-backed securities. Although Burry was proven correct, he does not claim unique prescience. In a speech in 2011, he states:

> As books and articles on the crisis proliferate it becomes clear that at nearly every failed institution and every relevant department of government, there was someone whose insight was every bit as good as mine, and in many cases better. However, none, zero, zero were in the top job.[10]

Burry puts the blame on CEOs and top government officials for not seeing the financial risk to the economy. Thus, numerous times some analyst at a firm had insights similar to Burry's. Perhaps this analyst kept it to himself for fear of looking stupid or spoke up and was dismissed. Either case is problematic and at the heart of what we are exploring in this book.

Burry's story helps to illustrate the capacity of independent thinking, which includes being a critical thinker. Critical thinking is a constellation of thinking habits that involve critique.[11] It includes a sensitivity to evidence, a willingness to question assumptions if they do not make sense, and a desire to reason through ideas and issues rather than accept superficial explanations. As the cognitive psychologist Daniel Willingham argues, critical thinking is intertwined with domain knowledge.[12] For example, it's difficult to critically evaluate a company's financial statements, if you've never learned the basics of accounting. Thus, critical thinking, while it can be a *propensity* to question superficial explanations, also requires some domain knowledge. Michael Burry needed to understand the mortgage underwriting process before he could question the long-term viability of the economy. Of course, many other people understood the mortgage process, but didn't see what Burry was seeing. It took much deeper digging and a willingness to question settled assumptions.

Of course, critical thinking can be taken to an extreme. Any proposition can be criticized, but it's the quality and rigor of the criticism that counts. Burry's investment thesis in 2006 could have been critically scrutinized—or any idea of an entrepreneur—in the name of critical thinking. It's ideas that withstand critical scrutiny and reasoned argument that are worthwhile. Thus, independent thinking is about both idea generation and effective idea selection. You need to generate original, independent thoughts, but also scrutinize those thoughts—effectively reasoning through some of your ideas without bluntly critiquing everything. As the Nobel Prize winning chemist Linus Pauling said when asked how he generates good ideas, "Well, you have to have a lot of ideas and throw out the bad ones."[13] In this manner, there is an evolution to our thinking: We create variation by generating ideas and then select those that are the strongest.[14] Figure 2.1 provides a visualization of this process.

While idea variation, selection, and evolution can occur in our own minds, it can certainly be social—as it is in the scientific community. We draw upon the ideas of others and are aided in their selection and refinement by the imagined and real critique of others, although when

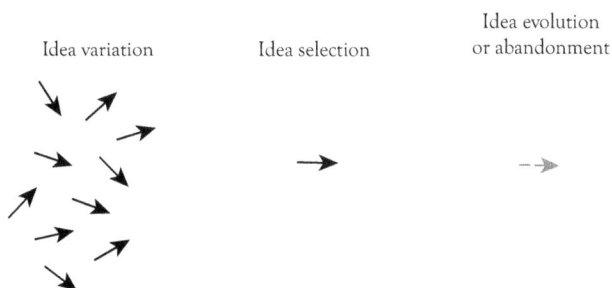

Figure 2.1 Idea variation, selection, and evolution

our ideas are critiqued through a social process, we risk the hazards of social conformity as we've explored. Burry's investment idea was harshly criticized, but it was able to withstand these criticisms (at least in his own mind) given the strength of his reasoning.

Effective idea selection is an important aspect of developing arguments that are well reasoned—not random thoughts. As Figure 2.1 visually depicts, we have opinions and ideas popping into our head all the time. We have to distinguish between opinions that are ill-informed and those that are grounded in an important value, evidence, or emotion. Through-out the interviews that informed this book, many participants mentioned the distinction between random thoughts and well-reasoned viewpoints. As one former CEO of a Fortune 500 company states:

> I think today, someone will…say, "Okay, I think we should do X." Okay, well why do you think we should do X? And then you realize that the person really hasn't thought through the idea very well…I think it becomes almost dangerous because it's not well-thought-out. It's just blurting stuff, and I don't find it particularly useful or compelling. I would rather if someone had an independent idea, they spend a couple of weeks and put together a three-to-five-page summary outlining an idea or a hypothesis, put some facts in there, and let's debate it a little bit. Let's really push against some of the assumptions, and I think unfortunately, the ability of people to express an opinion, again with maybe hardly any consequences or any facts behind it is not a good thing, actually.

Independent thinking involves more time and investment in the idea. It's not just blurting something out, but an idea that is well reasoned and developed.

This is complicated to distinguish in our own minds, however. We quickly form impressions, stories, and opinions on very little information. As the Nobel winning psychologist Daniel Kahneman states, "The remarkable aspect of our mental life is that we are rarely stumped."[15] We quickly develop opinions and perspectives on very little data and are often blind to what we don't know. This can lead to an irrational level of confidence that isn't warranted given our inexperience. This is most prevalent as we learn a new domain. There is often a "beginner's bubble," where a little knowledge leads to overconfidence in our perspective.[16] Think of learning about the stock market, for example. You have some knowledge, but you are blind to the complexity of evaluating stocks and how many skilled investors have developed strategies over decades and yet are only marginally successfully. This initial knowledge puts you on "Mount Stupid," in the words of the organizational psychologist Adam Grant.[17] You have an initial wave of overconfidence with your limited knowledge. Over time, your confidence diminishes as you realize a new domain is more complicated than you thought. If you persist, however, your accuracy and confidence can return to higher and more realistic levels. The problem with being on Mount Stupid is that it is hard to know you are on Mount Stupid. The ability to evaluate your incompetence develops with more expertise.[18] Thus, *effective* idea selection requires a platform of expertise.

However, to think independently requires expertise that is not entrenched in common ways of viewing the situation. To balance having expertise but being able to see things differently requires an ability to overcome what researchers call "cognitive entrenchment."[19] Cognitive entrenchment is having "a high level of stability in one's domain schemas," such that there is little flexibility in one's thought.[20] While domain expertise can lead to cognitive entrenchment, one factor that moderates this relationship is having a personal background that allows you to see multiple perspectives.[21]

Being able to bring multiple perspectives to any situation is aided by the variety of our background experiences. As we gain experience in life, in different social groups or domains, we can shift perspectives more readily. This was seen in the first chapter in the story of Tom, who saw the removal of performance ratings differently based on his prior experience at another company. He had access to a different social experience that allowed him to take multiple perspectives. As the management scholar Andy Hargadon, who studies innovation, argues, "People create novel insights by importing and recombining schemas and scripts learned in other contextual domains—in other words, people do not think out of the box, they think in other boxes."[22] Thus, by having a variety of experiences, we can "think in other boxes" and are less beholden to "cognitive entrenchment" based on singular expertise. A useful image that captures the competing tension of having domain expertise, but also having a variety of experiences is being T-shaped. You need relatively deep expertise in a domain, the vertical aspect of the T, but also a breadth of experience, the horizontal aspect of the T. If you only have vertical depth, you risk cognitive entrenchment. If you only have horizontal breadth, you risk having impoverished knowledge without the expertise to question settled assumptions.[23]

While a variety of experiences help us "think in other boxes," being on the periphery of a field helps us overcome the social forces within it. If you are at the center of a domain, you have a vested interest in preserving the status quo and are more likely to fully view the world within the dominant lens. Your social ties are also likely to be enmeshed within the dominant paradigm. As social network scholars argue, "The ties that bind can also be the ties that blind."[24] Being on the periphery, however, means you have domain knowledge but are less beholden to it, either socially or cognitively. This was certainly true for Burry; he was an outsider and far on the periphery of the investment community. It allowed him to see differently and not be blind to the assumptions of most investors and bankers on Wall Street.

The importance of having a wide variety of experiences and being at the periphery of one's field has also been found among prominent inventors. Dean Simonton, a psychologist specializing in creativity, completed a systematic review of the biographies of prominent inventors. He discusses many of the characteristics that facilitate creativity:

> Their educational achievements are sometimes uneven but varied, with a striking tendency away from conformity to a single way of looking at their discipline. They often study under more than one mentor and find inspiration among a diversity of predecessors. They may be either ethnically or professionally marginal, where this marginality enables them to see issues in a totally different light from the majority in their field. These and other antecedents of eminence all influence the developing creator, producing a person who can generate a more heterogeneous array of associative variations.[25]

These "antecedents of eminence" may be difficult to cultivate with intentionality, but they aren't out of reach. We can value and cultivate interests in a wide variety of fields, in a way that allows us to see our core domain from a variety of perspectives. By and large, the horizontal dimension of being T-shaped can be discounted as we face constant opportunity costs with our time; developing deep expertise seems like a safer bet. Simonton's finding of "marginality" also means we can forgo the assumption that if we aren't a core member of a field, we can't make a contribution. Being on the periphery, in some instances, can be a virtue, at least if we are aiming for independent thinking.

Thus, two key dispositions that support independent thinking are critical thinking and being (or thinking like) an outsider. I equate critical thinking with *effective* idea selection. It's not blindly accepting every proposition, nor immediately rejecting every unique idea, but reasoning through ideas, letting the strongest ideas survive (on their merits). This is aided by being able to take multiple perspectives, often the result of having a wide variety of experiences and being on the periphery of a domain where you are less beholden to the dominant logic.

Slow Hunches and Curiosity

As we look at Figure 2.1, however, ideas rarely emerge fully formed. We may occasionally have an "aha moment," but they result from much prior effort.[26] At the outset, our ideas are often a vague notion that something doesn't make sense, and our effort to understand and refine our ideas takes time. The writer Steven Johnson in his book, *Where Good Ideas Come From*, uses the term "slow hunches" to explain this process of being at the edge of discovery. Johnson describes how innovative ideas incubate and evidence gains over time. As he states:

> Most hunches that turn into important innovations unfold over much longer time frames. They start with a vague, hard-to-describe sense that there's an interesting solution to a problem that hasn't yet been proposed, and they linger in the shadows of the mind, sometimes for decades, assembling new connections and gaining strength....But that long incubation period is also their strength, because true insights require you to think something that no one has thought before in quite the same way.[27]

In the field of economics, the process of following "slow hunches" is what Richard Thaler describes as he and his colleagues would eventually revolutionize the field of economics to create the field of behavioral economics. Behavioral economics brings insights from psychology into standard economic questions such as savings and investment decisions. It is this work that eventually won Richard Thaler the Nobel Prize in economics in 2017, but it all started with noticing "anomalies" and following slow hunches. As Thaler describes:

> A slow hunch is not one of those "aha" insights when everything becomes clear. Instead, it is more of a vague impression that there is something interesting going on, and an intuition that there could be something important lurking not far away. The problem with a slow hunch is you have no way to know whether it will lead to a dead end.[28]

Beginning in the 1970s, Thaler was noticing cases where we fall short of the rational model of behavior. The rational model often describes our behavior but not always. We sometimes exhibit self-control, but in many situations we do not. We plan for the future but often fall short. The rational model of behavior sets a standard of what we *should* do, and this model was largely at the heart of economics. Thaler and colleagues, however, began adding descriptive realism into how we behave. For example, one of the signature programs developed from behavioral economics is Save More Tomorrow.[29] Save More Tomorrow starts with the insight that as our income increases, rather than save it, we'll likely spend it (i.e., we aren't perfectly rational). However, if you ask anyone, they will tell you they *should* save more when their income increases. Save More Tomorrow is an automatic plan to increase the percentage of savings from your paycheck when you receive a pay increase in the future. This intervention recognizes we will fall short of our intentions and helps us behave more rationally (i.e., in accordance with our long-term desires). It makes sense that we will fall short of our intentions for savings, but this kind of descriptive realism was largely absent from economics.[30]

Thaler, as an independent thinker, was critically questioning the assumptions of the rational model of behavior. As he tells the story, he was able to do this by drawing on insights from psychology, in particular, the work of Daniel Kahneman and Amos Tversky. This allowed him to take multiple perspectives and strengthen his "slow hunches" with evidence from psychology. He vividly describes his first forays into psychology in the late 1970s after a colleague suggested he read the work of Kahneman and Tversky. As he states:

> Having spent all my time in the economics section, I found myself in a new part of the library. I started with the duo's summary paper published in *Science*: "Judgment Under Uncertainty: Heuristics and Biases." At the time I was not sure what a heuristic was, but it turns out to be a fancy word for a rule of thumb. As I read, my heart started pounding the way it might during the final minutes of a close game. The paper took me thirty minutes to read from start to finish, but my life had changed forever.[31]

But what caused him to seek out insights and evidence from psychology in the first place? Part of the story for Thaler (and many others) is curiosity. Curiosity is a drive to make sense of the world, to dislike the experience of not knowing, and a sensitivity to things that don't "make sense."[32] Curiosity is a drive state, much like hunger or thirst, that motivates learning. In accordance, a colloquial way of describing curiosity is having a "hungry mind." In this way, a small priming dose can compel wanting to know more, and our curiosity is reduced once we have sufficiently explored a question. However, curiosity can also be self-propelling: the more we learn, the more we become interested in a topic—creating a virtuous cycle.

While curiosity is a state that we all experience, we also vary in our propensity to be curious. In this, we vary as to whether we'll allow ourselves to explore a "slow hunch" or something that doesn't make sense. We can either ignore the weak signals of our curiosity or more thoroughly explore our interests—with less concern for an immediate payoff. As Thaler mentions, "The problem with a slow hunch is you have no way to know whether it will lead to a dead end."[33] Dead ends and "rabbit holes" are only revealed in retrospect, after we've spent some time pursuing a line of inquiry. However, *being* curious is to be less preoccupied with avoiding "dead ends" or "rabbit holes" in advance. Thus, Thaler was willing to explore the field of psychology, wherever it might lead. This included, after reading the work of Kahneman and Tversky, spending a year at Stanford in the late 1970s after hearing they would be studying there.

Thaler continued following his curiosity to understand economic behavior that didn't "make sense" within the standard view of economic rationality. He recorded a list of anomalies in his office and eventually began writing a column on anomalies in an economic journal. The first one appeared in 1987 and Thaler opened the article with an epigraph from Thomas Kuhn's *The Structure of Scientific Revolutions*, stating that "Discovery commences with the awareness of anomaly, i.e., with the recognition that nature has somehow violated the paradigm-induced expectations that govern normal science."[34] This was a nonsubtle indicator that Thaler, as he later admitted in his 2015 memoir, was aware of his endeavor. The anomaly he first wrote about was the "January Effect" in stock markets, which was a higher monthly return in January compared to other months, in particular the first five days of the trading year. If stocks were perfectly priced based on all available information at any moment in time, as the prevailing theory argued, why would the January Effect exist? Thaler didn't offer an answer, but only refuted a current hypothesis about tax-loss selling and demonstrated how widespread the phenomenon was in other countries. He concluded the article with an open question, using the amusing phrase in German: "*Vas ist das?*" In a way, Thaler was trying to pique the curiosity of fellow economists, the same way his own curiosity led him to explore new psychological explanations for economic behavior. These columns were a success, with a large readership, and as Thaler recounts from many conversations with colleagues, these articles became their first introduction to behavioral economics.

While the column on anomalies helped him engage with the profession, he faced fairly persistent disdain and dismissal of his ideas from fellow economists, but it didn't deter him. And while curiosity and following slow hunches tell part of the story, Thaler was also, by nature, a nonconformist. He would recount the various decades of slowly making change in his 2015 memoir *Misbehaving: The History of Behavioral Economics*, and in an interview, he admits that "misbehaving refers not just to the people in economic models but to the author of this book."[35] In reflecting on his career after receiving the Nobel Prize, he also states:

> I am admittedly a rabble rouser who enjoys stirring the pot and challenging conventional wisdom. But taking on that role brings an emotional burden: it is not easy having economists you admire dismiss your research because it does not follow existing norms.[36]

In Thaler's story, we see a constellation of circumstances and personality dispositions that forged a new field. It would be too simplistic to say it was solely his curiosity, but curiosity and a willingness to follow "slow hunches" are a part of the story for anyone seeing (and pursuing) what others don't—from scientific discoveries to ideas that break the mold of deeply entrenched ways of thinking.

Although we may not have pretensions of scientific breakthroughs, the same mindset would be at work in exploring new emerging trends. Our curiosity—should we choose to listen to it—propels us to slowly gather evidence that strengthens, refutes, or refines our ideas.

Asking Questions and the Vulnerability of Looking Stupid

In addition to critical thinking, being an outsider, and curiosity, another key to independent thinking is being able to overcome the vulnerability of looking stupid. It is being willing to ask questions others aren't willing to ask. In doing so, you face the potential shame of being spoken to that you just don't "get it." One of the most dramatic examples of this is Sherron Watkins at Enron. Throughout the 1980s, Watkins, a Certified Public Accountant, worked for Arthur Anderson, a "Big 5" accounting firm. In 1993, she began working at Enron and in the summer of 2001 had been transferred to a new accounting division. In her new role, she was put in charge of 12 investments, and after getting up to speed, there were oddities that didn't make sense. As she recalls, "there was just a loss on the spreadsheet that made no sense to me, and when I kept asking and asking about these structures, I did not get good answers."[37]

What would become apparent was that executives at Enron had created shell companies where losses could be hidden and where these shell companies could "do business" with Enron. These were highly complex structures, and to Watkin's inquiring mind, they didn't make sense. As she recounts, "I hadn't practiced accounting in ten years, but you know, it just doesn't get that creative that you can just come up with some complicated structures and do business with yourself."[38] Watkins eventually wrote a six-page memo in August 2001 to Ken Lay, the CEO at the time, outlining the issues she was noticing and describing a plan of action. While she felt relieved about raising the issues with Ken Lay, that she had "done her duty," she would later find out that he would move to fire her behind the scenes. He decided against firing her based on legal counsel because a lawsuit about her dismissal might bring transparency to the practices she was questioning.

While the collapse of Enron at the end of 2001 is a complex tale of greed, corruption, and fraud, for our purposes, what led Sherron Watkins to be an independent voice? First, she had the background and expertise to think critically about what she was seeing. She understood accounting and was a CPA. This underscores the obvious point that we need a foundation of expertise to think independently. Just like 99 percent of us cannot walk into a theoretical physics conference and critique the mathematical formulas being discussed, we need one foot firmly within a domain to understand what is going on. To be independent, we also can't be consumed with being accepted by the group and be somewhat peripheral to it. Jessica Uhl, a mentee of Watkins at Enron, says gender played a role for Watkins speaking up. As Uhl states,

> Look at the management team: There's not a lot of female faces up there, and there never has been…Sherron's a vice president, so she's obviously not an outsider, but there is a dividing line there. If you're not part of the boys' club, maybe that makes it a little easier to take a big risk.[39]

In addition to expertise and peripheral group membership, having a secure sense of personal worth allows one to ask difficult questions. As Soloman Asch found in his conformity studies, independence is fostered by a secure sense of personal worth.[40] This allows you to face the pressure to conform and face the vulnerability of looking stupid. Watkins describes how she would ask questions and the responses implied that she was not smart enough to "get it."

> If you kept asking questions, they would really have this intimidating tone to their voice and say, you know, look we've hired the sharpest accountants and the sharpest finance minds in the country...the implication was you're really going to keep asking questions and show how stupid you are...so smart people just kind of got intimidated into not asking questions.[41]

Sherron Watkins was eventually vindicated in her questioning and was one of three women named "persons of the year" in 2002 by *Time* magazine as whistleblowers. Nevertheless, it was an enormously challenging experience, one filled with many sleepless nights. In retrospect, she now advises anyone in a similar situation to build peer support. As she states, "If folks run into Enron-like behavior, I always suggest finding peers who will join you in your quest to correct things. Never go it alone."[42] This mirrors what is found in experimental studies of conformity, which have found that having one ally dampens the fear of being independent and strengthens one's resolve.[43] It also makes your point of view harder to dismiss.

Another story (although less dramatic than the fall of Enron) that illustrates asking questions and the vulnerability of looking stupid was told to me by Steven. Steven openly questioned the forced ranking policy of his organization as the head of a subunit of a civil service organization of about 3,000 employees.[44] Each year, every subunit would rank all their employees on a forced curve, and they would then aggregate these forced rankings. In many years, there was adequate reason for people to be placed "below normal." However, this year in Steven's subunit, he says everyone was deemed to be a "good officer"; yet, given the policy of forced ranking, one of his officers was at risk of being ranked "below normal." Being ranked as below normal didn't mean automatic dismissal. A person needed two straight years of being ranked below normal to be put on a dismissal plan. Nevertheless, it was a black mark on someone's record and Steven didn't think this officer's performance merited such a statement.

Thus, in a management meeting in front of over 40 people, Steven spoke up and questioned the policy. In doing so, he was in the back row of seats, as he wasn't senior enough to be one of the 25 individuals sitting at the table in the room. In response, the head of the organization gave Steven "a very straight forward bureaucratic reply that this forced ranking exercise is something that every organization does, it's done at all levels, and too bad if somebody falls in there."

Steven needed to be more persistent. As he recalls, "I think that's the part where it prompted me then to ask the follow-up question because I could sense that if I didn't speak up, then this would naturally take its course." He says:

> The person who responded to me is actually the head of the organization, and his point is that this is a company policy. This is across the civil service, and I thought that if I simply accepted that, if I didn't respond, then it would simply be taken as "he asked a question, he was given a reply," and then the case is closed…That's why I then made a further appeal to say I understand the principle, and I can understand why there's such a policy set up within the organization. I said, "but still, there is a policy, and there is an intent," and I said, "that intent cannot be that even people who are doing well, and who contribute to the organization simply because of a policy of forced ranking now end up being put in a bucket of being a low performing officer."

For Steven to question this policy was highly unusual. As he states, "For someone who's actually sitting in the back bench, to stand up and ask a question, and not only do so, but persist in asking the question, despite being giving that answer, there was silence in the room." Steven didn't have an ally who spoke up to support him, but he did have the perception that many other individuals thought the same as he did. He says, "If you could see speech bubbles in people's heads…there are other people who quietly agree, but they are not going to speak up in that situation."

Steven's reason for persistence was partly the result of wanting to be "consistent" with the values he worked to instill in his 80-person unit. Within his unit, they had "woven logic, reason and principles into the way we work." These principles included advocating for vulnerable families. Steven says:

> We were an organization that helped vulnerable families, and our message to our officers is that you don't give up on the families. You try to learn what their circumstances are, and if the system doesn't…if the policy and the system doesn't fit it, then it is your duty to surface it, rather than to tell the family that you don't fall within the policy.

At issue was a desire to be consistent with the type of leadership he advocated for and to not blindly comply when the policy did not make sense.

> It just felt [like] the right thing, the natural thing to surface and raise this issue. I would expect that officer to advocate for vulnerables and families in the same way that I would, so in that sense, it's being as consistent as possible.

After Steven's persistent questioning, he was asked to submit his case for the officer in writing. This response highlights a key aspect of dissent. You may not, and are unlikely, to change anyone's mind immediately in the moment. For the head of the organization to grant an immediate exception to the forced ranking policy might make him look feeble in front of a large audience. Nevertheless, dissent sparks thinking that may not be evident in the moment. As Steven recalls,

> As I look back, I'm not sure if they agreed when my point was made, but they couldn't do it there and then. They didn't want to acknowledge it there and then, or they decided to have me provide written representation on it, and then they were convinced by what was written.

In the end, Steven's superiors did offer an exemption for his officer, but their decision to do so was a "black box," where Steven did not know what went into the process.

As Steven reflects on the incident, he describes how he made himself vulnerable by standing up for his employee. By questioning the policy of forced ranking, he faced the "vulnerability of looking stupid." As Steven states,

> because the way in which the head of the organization spoke to me, it's like, "this is a standard practice across all organizations, even the most senior leaders go through it," so it's kind of said in a way that makes you look very silly. It is like—how do you not get this?

This highlights a peril of independent thinking; you may be paternalistically scolded. It may be true that you do not understand some basic reason for a policy, and its explanation clarifies the issue for you. In the process, you may "look stupid." It's a risk. In other cases, you may have a valid point, and while you may not change minds in the moment, it may lead to positive change in the organization. Ultimately, Steven's story illustrates many of the factors that lead to being an independent voice. It dealt with an enduring value, asking questions as a means of dissent, and overcoming the vulnerability of looking stupid.

The Value Placed on Reason and Truth

Another value that sparks independent thinking is the value placed on reason and truth, which is how much an individual cares whether his or her beliefs are true and whether they are grounded in reasons that make sense.[45] Having a commitment to the truth is often contrasted with "getting along" and these two motives ("getting at truth" versus "getting along") often come into conflict.[46] For example, in one interview I conducted with a man named Gary, he described how truth was his highest value. As he states, "Commitment to learning/discovering the truth might be my deepest value—it's far more important to me than pain-avoidance, popularity, etc." Throughout Gary's life, he mentions being more of a "loner" and that he was "less oriented toward sort of maintaining social acceptance and gaining everybody's approval." He also developed an early fascination with science and eventually earned a doctorate in zoology. As Gary says, "I always want to know what the truth is, even if it's gonna be very painful, even if it has a cost, and I've noticed that a lot of people around me aren't that way."

This value placed on reason and truth at the expense of social acceptance would eventually lead Gary to speak up about research misconduct. In a research lab where Gary was working, he was analyzing data that led to different conclusions than the prior theories of the head of the lab. He says that because of this he was then forbidden to analyze the data on his own time. Furthermore, Gary suspected potential data fabrication by the head of the lab and was willing to speak up that he thought several data points were not accurate. As Gary recounts:

> When I whistle blew on the misconduct, nobody supported me.... Like even the grad students who had witnessed [the head of the lab] fabricating, told me that she was fabricating, they said, listen, if you report this, if we report this, what's gonna happen to our reputation? We've got publications on the line. Those will become suspect. So, basically, when I did that, I had to do it all alone.

When asked what made him speak up in contrast to other graduate students, Gary responded:

> Truth, man, truth. It's science. I've been a scientist—Okay, I've loved science ever since I was a kid. I've been a scientist my whole adult life. This cannot happen, and in my experience, it doesn't. And I've worked with a huge number of people over the years, and I've never witnessed anybody do this before.

Based on speaking up, Gary lost his research position and had to take a much lower paying temporary job. This illustrates that although we laud whistleblowers on the cover of *Time* magazine in cases like Enron, the more everyday form of whistleblowing can have devastating personal consequences. Ultimately, an investigation did not prove data fabrication;

However, after a lengthy investigation of the professor's conduct across many situations, the university dismissed the tenured professor and she resigned.

Along with the social and career costs of speaking up, Gary's story illustrates how the value placed on reason and truth is often embedded in a love of science, as was the case with Gary. But what is scientific thinking, exactly? It is a constellation of thinking habits and methods, aimed at getting at truth. By "truth," I mean explanations of the world that coincide with the best available reasons and evidence.[47] Sensitivity to evidence and a willingness to change one's mind based on evidence are central to a scientific mindset. As Lee McIntyre describes in his book *The Scientific Attitude:* "What is distinctive about science is that it *cares about evidence* and *is willing to change its theories on the basis of evidence.*"[48]

Along with a reliance on evidence, a scientific mindset views the world as intelligible. Thus, as Harvard linguist and psychologist Steven Pinker states, "In making sense of our world, there should be few occasions on which we are forced to concede, 'It just is' or 'It's magic' or 'Because I said so.'"[49] One can see how this mindset would clash with the dictates of following a boss's orders, especially of the variety "that's just how it's done" or "because I said so." Instead, a scientific mindset is about getting to the bottom of issues with a belief that they can be understood. We see this with the inquiring mind of Sherron Watkins and Gary's analysis of data. Gary, for example, wasn't content to view the data in accordance with the head of the lab, merely because she was an authority figure who had a vested interest in supporting her prior theories. Of course, fraud moves into a different territory beyond competing explanations for data. But to uncover fraud requires the same pursuit of truth one might engage in to evaluate scientific truth.

Having a high value placed on reason and truth also means you want to have strong reasons for what you think and believe.[50] For Gary, you can see the value placed on reason and truth is a "protected value." A "protected value" is a value that we are unwilling to make a trade-off for.[51] In this sense, it is a rule that should be followed regardless of the consequences. We can see this as Gary spoke up about potential data fabrication regardless of the difficulties he faced. Protected values also involve a moral obligation. In this way, there is little deliberation about what to do, but a moral imperative to uphold your protected value.[52]

The protected value of "truth" can also be seen among journalists as they aim to report the facts of a story. This value, and how it illustrates independent thinking, was evident among a group of journalists at Knight Ridder in the lead up to the U.S. invasion of Iraq in 2003. To briefly recount: Not long after the September 11, 2001 terrorist attacks, the Bush administration began making a case for war with Iraq. The administration sought to make a connection between the leader of Iraq, Saddam Hussein, and Al Qaeda, the terrorist group directly responsible for the September 11 attack. In addition, the Bush administration argued that Saddam Hussein had, or would imminently acquire, weapons of mass destruction (WMDs). The Bush administration would make these claims despite questionable intelligence. It would become clear over time that these two pretenses for war were wrong. There was no connection between Saddam Hussein and Al Qaeda, and Saddam Hussein did not have weapons of mass destruction.

During the lead up to the Iraq invasion, most media outlets diligently reported the administration's claims about Iraq without skeptically questioning their sources. A set of journalists—Jonathan Landay, Warren Strobel, and Joe Galloway—and newspaper editor, John Walcott, published dozens of stories that questioned the administration's claims.[53] As Walcott states:

> When the administration made an assertion, a lot of people wrote it down and printed it and we looked at it and said "that doesn't make any sense. Is that true?" And we proceeded to call people. And very often, and very quickly, people said "no, that's not true," or "there is no evidence that that's true," or "they left out part of the story."[54]

In the aftermath of September 11, there was pressure to conform, given the spirit of patriotism after a national tragedy. Thus, it became more difficult to be an independent voice against and within the administration. In addition, many journalists were more concerned about faithfully reporting information from their high-ranking source as a way to maintain relationships, rather than skeptically examining their arguments.

Walcott outlines the peril of falling into "pack behavior." As he states:

> Anyone who has covered a big story knows how easy it is to fall into pack behavior. You always worry that you don't have what the other guy has. It takes a strong constitution to ignore the pull of the crowd…Too many journalists, including some very famous ones, have surrendered their independence in order to become part of the ruling class.[55]

For Knight Ridder, their skeptical reporting proved to be accurate as no weapons of mass destruction were found in Iraq nor was a hidden program to create such weapons found either. Many of the claims that supported the administration's arguments were made by Iraqi exiles who had a strong desire to see Saddam Hussein ousted, making their claims questionable. Nevertheless, the unsupported claims of Iraqi exiles made their way into many prominent news outlets.

While Landay, Strobel, and colleagues weren't the only individuals questioning the rationale for war, they were nearly alone as journalists in reporting skeptical stories. It was a lonely position without social validation. As Strobel states, "There was a period when we were sittin' out there and I had a lot of late night gut checks where I was just like, 'Are we totally off on some loop here?'"[56]

Their skepticism proved true, but with any claim of independent thinking is the law of large numbers. With enough people making different claims, some people are bound to be correct, based purely on probability. But that assumes all guesses are equal. The Knight Ridder journalists, however, had clear reasons to doubt the evidence. As Jonathan Landay, himself, states, he thought Saddam Hussein had WMDs until he looked into the matter more thoroughly. He says:

> I simply spent basically a month familiarizing myself with what Saddam's weapons of mass destruction programs had been and what had happened to them. And, there was tons of material available on that from the UN weapons inspectors. I mean, they got into virtually everything, and their reports were online.[57]

In doing this background research, Landay changed his mind based on the evidence (or lack thereof) and outlined clear reasons that such a program would have been detected. Landay and his colleagues would write stories that questioned the vice president's claims that Saddam Hussein had resumed his efforts to acquire a nuclear weapon. As Landay wrote in September 2002 (several months before the invasion of Iraq in March 2003),

> The absence of intelligence pointing to a spike in the Iraqi threat contrasts sharply with Cheney's warnings that Saddam soon will have a nuclear bomb, could move on his neighbors or could supply a weapon of mass destruction to terrorists.[58]

Their stories, however, didn't gain much traction as Knight Ridder didn't have a voice in the newspaper markets of New York or Washington, DC. The stories produced by the Knight Ridder journalists could only run in 30 potential partnership newspapers in various cities throughout the United States. However, the newspapers could choose not to run the stories written by Knight Ridder, which they often did, especially because the Knight Ridder stories were not in line with the dominant narrative in many prominent media outlets. In 2013, Jonathan Landay was asked by a CNN news anchor: "How did it feel…to be the lone holdouts in this pursuit of truth and fact?" Landay responded: "'Lone holdout' is a good word because even some of our newspapers—we work for a chain of 30 newspapers. Even some of our own newspapers wouldn't print our own stories."[59]

In contrast to the journalists at Knight Ridder, the vast majority of high-profile media outlets were insufficiently skeptical in their reporting leading up to the Iraq invasion, including the *New York Times*. The *New York Times* even apologized to their readers for "coverage that was not as rigorous as it should have been…Looking back, we wish we had been more aggressive in re-examining the claims as new evidence emerged—or failed to emerge."[60] One factor that helped the Knight Ridder journalists get the story right was that they were, to some degree, outsiders to mainstream media outlets. They didn't rely on high-ranking sources, but instead did more painstaking work of speaking to mid-level government employees who would have less interest in conforming to the administration's narrative.[61]

The journalists at Knight Ridder would eventually win numerous awards for their reporting, especially as the Bush administration's claims for going to war were found to be inaccurate. These awards were recognized as early as the beginning of 2004 when they were honored for stories that discredited the claims that Iraq had tried to purchase uranium in Africa (a claim that President Bush had made in the State of the Union address).[62] With Knight Ridder's reporting, we see many of the hallmarks of independent thinking and how having a strong value placed on reason and truth helps one overcome the forces of conformity. They weren't content to simply recount the stories of those in charge, but skeptically examined claims asking if they were true. They felt the pull to conform and were concerned that they might be "off on some loop." While they did have the social validation of each other, they were largely alone among media outlets in their skepticism of the administration.

With both Gary and the journalists at Knight Ridder, we can see how a high value placed on reason and truth fosters independent thinking. We also see how "getting at the truth" conflicts with "getting along." As a protected value, it's unlikely Gary or the journalists at Knight Ridder deliberately chose to place truth and reason above "getting along." It's part of who they are. It helped them combat the forces of conformity, most directly by wanting to act in accordance with reasons and to not passively accept dogma, tradition, or authority as a standard for one's beliefs and actions. For both Gary and the Knight Ridder team, it didn't matter that an authority was making certain claims. They didn't accept what they were being told by an authority; they needed stronger reasons to ground their beliefs.

Professional Integrity and Constructive Deviance

In addition to the characteristics we've seen, through many of the interviews, the reason for sharing an independent point of view was to act with integrity, meaning there is congruence between what we think and how we act.[63] When there is a lack of congruence, this leads to a sense of dissonance that we seek to reduce.[64] But if there is incongruity between what we really think and the situation we are in, what is the source of what we "really think?" In the cases I explored, the source was often professional norms. Thus, *professional* integrity seems salient as a motivating force for dissenting. This is particularly true when someone's self-concept is highly integrated with their profession. Professional norms can be more loosely established such as the role of human resources in an organization, or more professionally codified, as they were in one example of an actuary that I interviewed.

Mark was early in his career as an actuary at a small office in the Pacific Northwest. In his firm, there were three owners, one in Mark's office of 25 individuals, and two in a larger office on the East Coast. Over the course of time, Mark began noticing "sloppy work" that he "surmised was the result of understaffing and not attention to what you would call peer review and short deadlines." Mark spoke up about one critical error he found to the head of the office. He recalls, "I went in and I had this conversation. He just basically said, 'They'll never know about it. We'll fix it next year. I'm glad you caught it. Just don't worry about it.'" Mark's willingness to speak up was informed by wanting to maintain professional integrity to the standards of the American Actuarial Association. As he says, "It sets the standards for practice." In this way, adherence to the norms of the profession created a platform for speaking up to his boss. As Mark states:

> There's no question the standard of the profession creates a platform that allows you to stand on there and make this kind of assessment. Because it's part of the standards of practice, it's part of the testing procedures, it's part of the practice procedures, you have a little bit of a platform then…It helped me think this through, so it wasn't just [Mark] against this guy. It was like, no, there's a professional standard here.

Thus, Mark was appealing to a higher set of norms for professional conduct, rather than the norms set by the head of his office. This gave him a platform to stand on in speaking up.

In addition to Mark appealing to the norms of his profession, he and others in the office would learn that the head of the office was having an affair with a secretary. This, along with the poor quality of the work, sparked Mark to contact the co-owners of the firm on the East Coast.

He had met them several times and wasn't afraid to do so. In recalling the experience, Mark thought little was going to change, and the co-owners didn't seem to want to make changes as long as revenue was being created. Not long after contacting the other co-owners, the head of Mark's office spoke to him privately and offered him a third of his share of the company. In response, Mark decided to resign. As he recalls, "I just said, 'You know what? I'm out of here.' I probably gave a couple weeks' notice. I was so disgusted." Here we see the emotion of disgust that partly compelled a resignation. It was disgust for the leadership of the office and not wanting to be associated with the organization any longer. Mark is also quick to mention that he had no family obligations or mortgage, and he was early in his career. This allowed him to resign without these considerations and without a clear plan. He would, however, quickly land on his feet at a larger, more prominent accounting firm in several months' time, but he doesn't know what he would have done if he was the sole breadwinner of a family.

Along with these contextual factors, Mark's story helps illustrate the importance of appealing to a higher set of professional norms and how they provide a platform for speaking up. Appealing to an alternative set of norms is central to what researchers call "constructive deviance." Constructive deviance is defined as "behaviors that deviate from the norms of the reference group such that they benefit the reference group and conform to hypernorms."[65] In Mark's case his "constructive deviance" of speaking up to raise the standards of the firm would benefit the firm (if he was listened to), and the "hypernorms" were the professional standards of actuaries.[66] Hypernorms, in other contexts, could be standards for human rights as outlined by the United Nations or what is considered legal and ethical in a society.[67]

Appeals and knowledge of hypernorms help provide a foundation for critique in speaking up in various contexts. This would be true when we are members of various subcultures (e.g., both professional and functional); it would also be true as we traverse in and out of various international cultures. For example, without an appeal to "hypernorms," our perspective might be to accept every business practice in any country as "just the way they do things." However, there might be wide-scale bribery or violations of basic fairness and human rights in the working conditions of a factory. Hypernorms, in these cases, provide a grounding for dissent (especially when these practices have not been codified into a country's laws). Thus, in constructive deviance, you deviate from your immediate reference group and appeal to this higher set of norms. As mentioned in the first chapter, you might then argue that you are not thinking independently, but merely being a conduit for hypernorms in your current context. That is true, but as defined, you are an independent voice in your current context, as we could never fully disentangle our thinking from the norms of the groups and experiences that shape us.

In Mark's retelling of his experience, we see how "professional integrity" and appealing to professional norms serve as a platform for speaking up. He acted with integrity to a set of "hypernorms"—in his case, professional actuary standards.

Mark's experience was similar to another story (from Amy) of speaking up about a factory manager deciding to put computer chips in all the lanyards of employees. In Amy's case, she didn't have norms as codified as actuaries, but instead her role included responsibility for culture and change management. As Amy says, one of the divisions in the company had a leader who was very "command and control" with a culture that was based on "fear." The head of the division wanted to have computer chips on every employee lanyard. The stated goal was just wanting the "data" and to "manage workflows," but Amy was skeptical, of course, and also heard of more invasive reasons for the technology. As she mentions:

> In a command-and-control environment, where they're managing every minute…what our supervisors immediately went to…"Oh, we can tell when people are taking smoke breaks, or if they're spending too long in the bathroom, or if…their lunch is too long. Or if two people are together that shouldn't be."

As the initiative was being considered, Amy spoke up in subtle ways in a weekly staff meeting with a senior executive. This executive had authority over the division considering the lanyards. She said, "I don't think this is a great idea. I think there's some real concerns." And that "I think you really need to think about how employees are going to receive this information." However, the initiative was moving forward and at one meeting, Amy got really "upset," which was unusual for her. She said:

> This is the wrong move. [The division leader] has created an organization that is, is sick. And these are employees who already feel micromanaged. And now you're going to put a dog collar on them…If you think that's going to help productivity, you're kidding yourself. And by the way, there's a ton of research that shows when your engagement goes down, your safety goes down. When you got employees worried about…getting tracked in the bathroom, do you think that they're going to be also focusing on their safety?

Amy says she was "a little impassioned" and that this initiative "felt so wrong to me." She further argued by saying, "You talk about treating employees like adults, you talk about respecting people, this doesn't really live up to any of that." The division leader wasn't in the room, and there was some silence after her final plea, but the senior executive, who advocated for "radical candor" thanked Amy for her "opinion" and the initiative went ahead.

Amy says, "I felt like I had to say something, or it was like malpractice from a change perspective." And that "I just felt like a moral duty to speak up…I felt like I needed to be on the record almost." Here we see her role—as an advocate for culture and change management—serving as a grounding for speaking up. The role aligns with a concern for the well-being of employees, and for Amy, it aligned with her professional identity, which led to her insistence that it would be "malpractice" and it was a "moral duty" to speak up. As Amy continues:

> You were asking me to be at that table wearing a change and culture hat to bring that expertise to the table. And so it did feel like it was almost my responsibility…I was there for that primary reason. And so I think I thought…I need to fulfill that duty.

While fulfilling a role facilitated speaking up, it was also about basic human dignity. Amy says her use of the term "dog collars" was intentional in that they were "treating people like animals." Thus, the hypernorms of trust and respect for individuals were enmeshed in her desire to fulfill her duty to her role. Over time, Amy felt validated in her concerns. The product received an ethics complaint, among others, about tracking while using the restroom, and the division leader was eventually removed from his position for creating a "toxic culture." For Amy, she was "glad" she spoke up, even though it didn't change the outcome, and she doesn't think wording her appeal differently would have helped. Similar to Mark's story of speaking up about the poor quality of work in his accounting firm, we see how Amy's role in change management served as a grounding for dissent. In this way, we can see how awareness and integrity to professional norms provides a platform for speaking up.

Summary

Over the course of this chapter, we have seen many dispositions and values that help promote independent thinking. These include:

1. Thinking critically and having the domain knowledge to question assumptions
2. Thinking like an outsider and taking a variety of perspectives
3. Being curious and willing to follow "slow hunches"
4. Having a secure sense of personal worth that allows you to question assumptions and potentially "look stupid"
5. Having values that encourage reasoning and a sensitivity to evidence about what is "true," often embedded in a scientific mindset
6. Maintaining professional integrity and appealing to a higher set of "hypernorms" in a current context

Importantly, all of these dispositions and values can be cultivated. None of them are ways of thinking that we are born with. We can develop our domain expertise, and thus our ability to critically evaluate claims and perspectives. Within limits, we can broaden our understanding of a wide variety of fields, thus allowing us to see our domain from different perspectives. We can follow our curiosity and "slow hunches." We can take risks to ask questions when something doesn't make sense, even if we might look "stupid" in the process. We can value reason, truth, and evidence to determine our perspective, and we can act with professional integrity when we are in situations where professional norms are violated. All of these can be facilitated if we are an outsider to the mainstream group, which dampens our desire to conform, as we saw with Michael Burry and Sherron Watkins, among others, although "being an outsider" is less of something to cultivate in comparison to the dispositions and values. Nevertheless, we can build our expertise, knowledge, and social networks in various domains such that we can bring many perspectives to an issue and "see" it like an outsider (i.e., not being "cognitively entrenched").

Now that we have seen ways to cultivate your capacity to speak up, *how* you do so is also important, which is the topic we turn to next.

CHAPTER 3

Persuading Without Authority

Throughout the stories of speaking up, it understandably emerged that *how* individuals spoke up was important. Many individuals had nuanced ways they thought about the process. These were necessary especially without formal authority, which is the authority granted to an individual in an organizational hierarchy. In many respects, one of the most critical components of our persuasiveness in any situation is whether we have formal authority. If we do not have formal authority as a result of our position, then we must use informal means of persuasion. Thus, persuasion through how we communicate and how we build credibility is essential. The following chapter will explore examples of being an independent thinker without formal authority and considerations in being persuasive with our ideas.

Emotional Regulation and Speaking Up

Throughout several of the interviews, it emerged that one key to effectively voicing an independent point of view is being able to regulate your emotions. In many instances, what provokes a different point of view is an emotional response, often anger. Anger, if it is appropriately harnessed, can instigate prosocial change; however, at an extreme level, it can be ineffective in persuasion. In a "dual threshold" model of anger regulation, the researchers Deanna Geddes and Ronda Callister discuss two "thresholds" of anger.[1] The first threshold is moving from "suppressed anger" to "expressed anger." The intensity of anger impacts whether the situation crosses this threshold as well as an individual's average level of emotional expressiveness. "Expressed anger" can lead to positive outcomes if it doesn't cross the "impropriety threshold," toward what Geddes and Callister call "deviant anger." Deviant anger might be where you lose your temper or express outrage in a meeting. The problem with "deviant anger," as Geddes and Callister argue, is that you become the source of attention rather than the issue itself.

This was painfully evident for one individual I interviewed who lost her temper in a meeting. Sarah, who was a senior executive at a professional services firm, recalls being frustrated with trying to compel action and she reached her boiling point. As she states, "I really kind of lost my shit to be honest. I was like, 'Why don't you people do anything?' I mean I basically screamed at them." This approach was ultimately ineffective, but as Sarah recalls:

> I had tried up to that point to say things forcefully, tactfully, truthfully. I also tried this approach of being very honest. Like, "I'm afraid we're going to lose the business guys. I need some help"… And none of these various approaches were really working, and the freakout approach didn't really work either, but it felt good for a few minutes.

Sarah's outburst was retold in one department, where she became a "folk hero" because of it. This makes the case that "deviant anger" makes *you* the focal point, rather than causing people to rethink their point of view based on your argument.

As we think about anger and making a persuasive message, there are two keys: it is important to be able to downregulate anger in keeping it from becoming too extreme (and crossing the "impropriety threshold") and not *always* suppressing anger, thereby losing the potential for action. Broadly speaking, this process of emotional regulation refers to "attempts to influence which emotions one has, when one has them, and how one experiences or expresses these emotions."[2] Emotional regulation is knowing when to suppress, amplify, or maintain your current emotional state.

The effort to downregulate anger to keep it from crossing the "impropriety threshold" was evident with Paul who discussed leading an international trip with graduate students. Each year, Paul and the students would visit the U.S. Consulate in a foreign country to learn about the country's politics and economy. In the past, these meetings had been educational and productive, but a different representative met with the students in their most recent trip. Over the course of the meeting, the U.S. representative became "less professional," making fun of international tourists and discussing how popular Donald Trump was in the country. He continued on, as Paul recalls:

> Then he kind of went on a rant where he said, and you know, in the US, we love international students, because we love all the extra tuition money you pay. And he was talking about that in a very disrespectful way. And the students were very uncomfortable at that point. You could just see kind of the expressions on their face and the eye rolling and I was really uncomfortable as well. And I was really struggling with not wanting to be disrespectful, but like, how do you address that? You know, do I say something? Do I not?

Paul even contemplated walking out of the meeting but thought it would be too extreme. At the end of the meeting, Paul went up to the representative and said "that was the most unprofessional meeting I have ever been in, just in terms of the tone and what was said, I said, it was really unprofessional. I'm just disappointed. I'm surprised."

The students then gathered in the lobby and were "upset." One international student was even in tears given she was also having a difficult time gaining employment in the United States and this was the "straw that broke the camel's back." Among the 20 to 25 graduate students, many of them were international students, as the graduate school had a large percentage of foreign students. This information had even been conveyed to the U.S. representative prior to the meeting as Paul thought it would be helpful to understand the audience.

Apparently, during the meeting with the U.S. representative, the students could see Paul was visibly upset. As one student commented, "He's like, wow, you were pissed. Like, he could see it on my face." While normally mild-mannered, Paul was trying to keep his emotions in check. As he describes, "I was trying to regulate the emotions by not using a swear word…you know, so I kept using the word that was so 'unprofessional.' So I was trying to modulate it, to stay within bounds."

Not long after the meeting, Paul had a long flight to another country and decided to write an e-mail to the individual (cc'ing the individual's boss). He also forwarded it to the students

> because I wanted the students to know…we're not letting this go by that, that, you know, they needed to be called out on it. And it had bothered me. And I think I was a little mad, maybe at myself, that I didn't say something in the meeting in the moment.

In reflecting on what to write in an e-mail Paul states,

> I think the other thing that was helpful was having a little bit of distance and time…when you go up to that person in the moment, you may not be able to phrase things, maybe as diplomatically, or as professionally.

In the e-mail Paul mentioned that "Several of the comments made were unprofessional and glib. There were many stereotypes used about 'Chinese tour groups'…that reflected badly on the State Department." He also outlined the value that the graduate school places on having a high percentage of international students and that "You made a glib point about all the money the U.S. earns from admitting foreign students who pay full tuition." The response from the representative was short, both after the meeting when Paul confronted the official and from the e-mail. The official apologized and admitted that he was using a "snide tone."

Abstracting from Paul's experience, we can see the challenge he faced in downregulating his anger—keeping it from crossing the "impropriety threshold." It's a universal challenge, as anger is often the emotional spark that compels us to share our viewpoint, but if anger becomes too extreme, our behavior becomes the central focus, rather than our message. As Paul reflects about the challenge, he shared how he struggled with expressing himself:

> How do you then go up and do that in-person in a way that's not disrespectful? So even for me, I was thinking about, how do I do this in a professional way? Because I'm getting on this person for being disrespectful and unprofessional so then shouldn't I have to take a higher road and do that in a more respectful way?

This is the challenge with regulating anger and working to appropriately harness it. At the same time, Paul was mad at himself for not saying something in the moment, which illustrates that we may suppress our anger too much to avoid acting unprofessional. It is a balance and a challenge to effectively voice our perspective in the moment in a way that doesn't cross a threshold of impropriety.

One way to help downregulate your emotions is by viewing the situation as a way to express your values but not aiming for immediate conversion or consensus. For example, one study examined the level of cardiovascular threat from being a lone dissenter. In the experiment, participants were told they would be the first person to give a two-minute speech about a controversial topic (government health insurance). Among participants, a subset was told they'd be giving the speech to four individuals holding opposite views. Cardiovascular threat was measured in multiple ways, including one's heart rate and cardiac output, which are physiological indicators of threat perception. The researchers then framed the goal of the speech in two different ways: either as a means to "express your opinions and demonstrate your core values" or that the goal of group discussion was to "reach a group opinion that you all agree on."[3] Among the subset of individuals speaking to people who help opposite views, the researchers found that if individuals were told the goal of group discussion was to "demonstrate your core values," the level of cardiovascular threat reduced compared to "reaching a group opinion you all agree on."

Importantly, the threat response can occur when the demands of the situation are viewed as exceeding your resources to meet those demands.[4] As you might imagine, you're more likely to have a sense of threat if you are told you need to get a group of individuals holding different views to come to a position that "you all agree on." In contrast, if the situation is framed as a means to "demonstrate your core values," the demands of the situation are lower and threat perception is diminished. Of course, this framing is not always effective if your goal is to get everyone to consensus; but by moderating your goal to be about "demonstrating your values," you can at least create a sense of dissonance in the group by breaking conformity. This dissonance may not result in immediate and public reversals of positions by any member of the group, but it can sow the seeds of doubt.

In addition to controlling your threat perception, knowledge of emotional regulation has been found to improve your effectiveness in speaking up. In one research study of 100 employees in an optometry company, having knowledge about how to emotionally regulate was measured along with the frequency of speaking up. In the study, to measure one's knowledge of emotion regulation, they used the Situational Test of Emotion Management, which presents short scenarios from which you need to choose the most appropriate course of action.[5] For example, one scenario asks the following question:

> Alan helps Trudy, a peer he works with occasionally, with a difficult task. Trudy complains that Alan's work isn't very good, and Alan responds that Trudy should be grateful he is doing her a favor. They argue. What action would be the most effective for Alan?
> (a) Stop helping Trudy and don't help her again.
> (b) Try harder to help appropriately.
> (c) Apologize to Trudy.
> (d) Diffuse the argument by asking for advice.

If you answered "d," you'd match the response of two-thirds of a panel of professionally trained psychologists (with another 17 percent choosing "a" and 8 percent choosing either "b" or "c"). In the study, if you scored better on the emotional regulation test *and* were rated as regularly speaking up, you also had better performance evaluations.[6] As Adam Grant, the researcher of the study says, it is being able to "rock the boat, but keep it steady." In this way, you aim to appropriately express your position, not letting your anger cross the "impropriety threshold," and in a way that can slowly change minds given the strength of your conviction.

Tactics to Persuade Without Authority

In addition to the overarching skill of emotion regulation, let's look at specific tactics and considerations in speaking up at work, starting with our level of directness.

Asking Questions Versus Being Direct

One way to effectively speak up and do so in a way that minimizes immediate defensiveness is to ask questions. We saw this in the previous chapter with Sherron Watkins at Enron where the process of dissent was through asking questions rather than bluntly stating a point of view. Asking questions has several advantages as an approach. First, we can learn something we didn't already know. That's relatively obvious, of course, but it signals an open-mindedness and willingness to learn. Second, in the minds of others, asking questions can help them connect the dots for themselves. Perhaps this won't happen immediately, but over time other individuals may come to understand your point of view. This delayed effect occurs because, by and large, individuals won't immediately reverse a position, especially publicly. We would lose "face" and may have a vested interest in the status quo or be closely identified with a position. We also don't want to be a person who immediately shifts our mind—who is a "flip-flopper."[7] Asking questions, however, can instill some doubt in others and get them to think differently over time. This was the approach one interviewee took as she tried to change the hiring practices of her firm.

Karen, a consultant in a small consulting firm, described her experience of trying to change the hiring process. She says that based on past failures in hiring, they had "locked down [their] selection process." As she explains:

> So, we don't have a lot of false positives anymore. People who get into the firm generally do well, but we're also probably not adding enough talent to the firm, or as much as we might need to be long-term sustainable. So, I have wondered if we are turning away people who could be successful because we've gotten so closed about what we think good talent looks like. This is something that has been core to who we are. It has been my boss's purview… Challenging how we do things in this space is challenging how my boss does his job, and that's uncomfortable.

Karen was newer to the firm and didn't want to be "overly critical" of her boss. As she says, "I was hopeful that people would at least consider an alternate point of view and filter it into their thinking." Karen describes her approach of indirectly raising questions. She says, "I had multiple conversations with my boss where I would share an observation and maybe raise a question, 'Hey, I've noticed this, this, this. I wonder if that, that, that.' Just to see if I could seed the discussion."

Karen received the usual resistance that they didn't have the organizational time and resources to change the way they were hiring and how detrimental it is when someone didn't succeed. Nevertheless, she thought the criteria were too narrow and wouldn't allow them to grow as they planned. When Karen was giving an internal presentation at her firm, she was asked about her biggest concern, and she discussed the need to expand the criteria in hiring. To make her message more "palatable," she describes her approach:

> I phrased it as an, "I wonder." "I've seen this. I know this. I had this conversation with so-and-so who told me this about the market, and I wonder what that means for X." So rather than being declarative, saying, "I think that means we need to change." I think I presented some facts and raised a question that they can all ponder on their own. So that the next time we talk about it, there's some thinking that's been done.

At the time of our interview, Karen says,

> I think there's an awareness that we are going to have to look at it differently. I don't know the level of appetite for making that change and if they're willing to make it next year or three years from now, but I would say my sense coming out of that last conversation was an acceptance that it is true or could be true.

Her message and tactic of raising questions is one aimed at slowly changing minds. In this way, individuals may slowly rethink their position. This approach helps counter motivated and defensive reasoning. If she was more declarative in her arguments, it might provoke immediate counterarguments that can strengthen the current attitude (e.g., the backfire effect).[8] By being direct, it can be more threatening, particularly if your senior manager views you as questioning his or her competence.

The approach of asking questions also helps avoid reprisal from her boss if he is not amenable to the suggestion. Indirect speech can solve a problem by offering you *plausible deniability* that you don't really think you should take a course of action.[9] "I was *just* asking the question!"— you might respond if it leads to immediate defensiveness and rebuttals. Thus, being indirect and asking questions of others can be a useful persuasion tactic, especially when you have no formal power. But is this always true? Can being direct have its advantages?

In examining this question, one research study compared the relative impact of "voice directness" and "voicer credibility" on managerial endorsement.[10] The researchers wanted to know whether you are better off asking questions or being more direct. In favor of more directness is that you'll be clearer with your point of view. There will be less ambiguity about what you think. In our prior example, Karen might have been too subtle with her questions, and her boss might have thought she was vaguely wondering if a change should be made. In contrast, asking questions is less threatening and might slowly change minds.[11]

The researchers collected a sample of 124 voice episodes from 53 participants and 33 managers from a health care support services company.[12] They measured directness by asking a manager if an employee is "direct," "clear about what he desires to improve," and "straightforward and to the point." They measured managerial endorsement with questions such as "This subordinate's suggestion has been, is being, or will be implemented" and "This subordinate's recommendation is valuable." The researchers found that directness itself was associated with greater managerial endorsement. This was also aided, as you might expect, by employee credibility. So, this research found that with their *specific* sample and set of measures, that directness had positive associations for promoting change.

So, should you be less direct, like Karen, or more direct, as this study found? As in most cases, the particulars of the situation needed to be accounted for. One metaphor that can help is thinking of our beliefs as a Jenga tower.[13] If you've never played the game, Jenga is a tower built from small blocks of wood and players take turns slowly removing blocks. A player loses the game by removing a block that causes the tower to come crashing down. Imagine our beliefs as a set of building blocks, with the base of the tower being fundamental assumptions that we strongly identify with and those at the top being lightly held beliefs. If we're making a recommendation for improvement near the top, we can be more direct. We want to be clear in our suggestions. If we're lower on the Jenga tower, and questioning deep-seated beliefs, we are better off slowly suggesting changes that can instill some doubt.

In an interview with Will, he took the direct approach with his boss. However, he was lower on the Jenga tower where his boss' sense of competency was directly implicated by his suggestions for improvement. When Will started in his job, his boss gave him a talk, "a big speech. And he said, 'I want you to be completely honest with me. Tell me how things are. I really want to know the truth on things." His boss, as it turns out, was also asked for complete honesty from a senior executive. However, when Will's boss had given some feedback to this senior executive, it wasn't received well. Therefore, Will's boss said, "I'm never gonna take offense to honest feedback."

Will noticed that the HTML format his boss had created for training wasn't the industry norm. As Will says, "Nobody else did it that way." Instead, a PowerPoint deck with attached documentation, along with learning objectives, would help participants focus. Will told his boss about this in a private conversation. As Will recalls, "I said, 'Listen, we can't keep doing it this way…It's really hard to get people to focus. And you know, we got to change everything you're doing. You need learning objectives." Will recalls:

It wasn't right away that he got offended…he kind of took it in, but then he just got kinda, I don't know, he was a big critic of everything I did. And even my two coworkers noticed it right away.

After this initial conversation Will backed off and didn't pursue the issue further. A few months passed and his boss wanted him to create the training for a new product, and said, "do it in your way," in a tone that to Will was "real kind of condescending." Will ultimately redesigned the format and impressed his fellow co-workers. However, his boss was still "offended" and "never really gave me any credit." Will says that his feedback ultimately "ruined that relationship with my boss."

For Will, the lesson was: "I wasn't an ass when I said, 'we're doing it wrong,' but I needed to really soften it. And I should have brought in more examples of the way it could work." Will also mentions he could have complimented some aspects of how they were doing things and how to incorporate those things into the new model. Ultimately, Will says, "I didn't pitch it well." In Will's situation, he was too direct, at least from the perspective of his boss, and the feedback he gave ruined the relationship.

As Ethan Burris, a management professor who has studied how to effectively sell your ideas, says, you need to "understand your manager's insecurities."[14] Burris argues that many managers are insecure about their ability to lead, which causes them to give more negative evaluations to employees who speak up. In one study, he found that as managers decreased by one-point on a confidence scale (out of five), they were 35 percent less likely to solicit advice from direct reports.[15] Thus, understanding if your manager has a lower sense of confidence is an important consideration in your approach.

In many situations, we may start off indirectly with "soft advocacy" and move to more direct appeals. As illustrated in Figure 3.1, this is a preferred route of persuasion because you can first get feedback on your ideas before potentially damaging a relationship.

Moving from "soft advocacy" to more direct appeals was the case for one woman I interviewed named Ellen. Ellen worked in the leadership and talent development group of a large organization, and they were developing a leadership experience for the top 70 to 100 people in the organization. However, there wasn't an easy way to get the exact list of people that should be considered. They started by looking at the data, but there was no consistency in titles. It wasn't possible to say here are "the four criteria for people that are at the top of the house." Thus, her department started "defaulting" with the perspective that "we know who the people are."

	Boss amenable to suggestion	Boss not amenable to suggestion
Directly challenge	Positive change made	Con: Potential reprisal and/or damaged relationship. Pro: Strength of conviction helps prompt change.
Indirectly challenge (*i.e. asking questions*)	Positive change made	Pro: Feedback helps shape approach in the future. Pro: Plausible deniability of position.

Move from indirect to direct challenges.

Figure 3.1 Outcomes of direct versus indirect challenges

For Ellen, part of the problem was that everyone would acknowledge unconscious bias, but when choosing individuals for the leadership development program, the perspective was "we just know who the people are." As she described, you get "the same people getting asked and certain people being overlooked and like, there are equity issues." Ellen wanted some documentation and objective standard for who would be chosen, rather than just picking the individuals that came to mind that run the organization. For her, and related to cognitive bias, "if we believe that our brains can be flawed, then let's act that way."

As Ellen describes, she tried a "soft advocacy" approach of determining who would be chosen. She first started with the tactic that they should "at least document our thinking." For Ellen, there had to be "something we can point to later and say, here's how we made our decision. Even if it's a little wiggly, right?" Ellen's soft advocacy was "trying to lead the conversation toward, in this case, more concrete criteria or to try to be the documenter." However, between meetings, other people would get the spreadsheet and pare it down to "the people we really should consider." Ellen didn't think this was nefarious; she had just been around long enough in the organization that she felt like it was time to "call ourselves on it."

After this soft advocacy, it eventually led to Ellen "putting her foot down." As she says, "I really kinda freaked out at my boss." "He specifically had taken the spreadsheet and done some stuff to it and kind of said,

'Oh, you know, I shortcutted our work, you know…I made a bunch of selections.'"

I just said,

Hey, you know, we've talked about this, and I just kind of put up a stop sign. And, let him know how uncomfortable I was. And, that it wasn't personal, and that it was sort of hitting a value spot.

Ellen had worked with him for many years and there was trust between them. Her supervisor eventually apologized a week later, given the strength of their relationship. However, an objective set of criteria proved to be elusive, and instead of making their own selections, they went to various departments and asked, "When I describe the kind of person we want in this program, who would it be there [in that department]?" In this way they tried to "reverse engineer the criteria." While this didn't completely remove bias, it could help create a broader set of individuals to be considered. In Ellen's story, we see how soft advocacy was ultimately unsuccessful, and for her it was an "integrity" issue. This led to more direct challenges that were helpful in communicating the strength of conviction she had about the issue. For Ellen, her directness was helpful in creating a less biased process.

As we can see in Figure 3.1, if you directly challenge your boss, if they are amenable to your suggestion, then a change will be made, but if they are not, you face potential reprisal, a damaged relationship, and perhaps a reputational hit, as was the case with Will. Thus, in many circumstances, it's better to start with indirect challenges and questions before being more direct in your approach.

Some situations, however, you may be speaking up in a domain that is so deeply held that being subtle is likely to be ignored and being direct will evoke defensiveness, or worse. Think of most whistleblowers or those trying to create social change against powerful vested interest. In these situations, an independent thinker can be effective in changing views, but it takes time and is often a difficult road. It depends on the depth of your conviction and the strength of the evidence of your viewpoint. In these cases, as whistleblowers experience, you may be shunned, dismissed, or worse.[16] The directness of your approach will depend on your personal calculus and willingness to engage in conflict.

Presenting Evidence

Helping people see your point of view through asking questions can also be important when presenting evidence. It helps to present the evidence in a neutral way to help individuals connect the dots and persuade *themselves*.

This was the case for Teresa who worked at a large, multinational manufacturing company and was the R&D engineering lead. She was sent to South America to research and gather consumer feedback on a fragrance product. After many days of talking with consumers about the product, she became convinced that this product had "no legs." Many of the consumers she spoke to wanted the fragrance product to have additional benefits. Teresa also observed the openness of most homes which wouldn't contain the fragrance indoors, and, she reasoned, most of the consumers had limited disposable income making this a product few would buy.

A few days after she returned, Teresa had a meeting with the marketing team, supply team, and several others where they discussed the product and she presented her research. However, she was the only one that was saying the product was a bad idea. As she recalls,

> But marketing, they just felt so strongly about moving forward with the project. And I was the only one who, who kind of was telling them "No, this is a terrible, terrible idea." And, we left the meeting and nothing changed, we were still going to move forward with the project.

After the meeting, several people came up to Teresa to say, "Wow, that was such a courageous thing you did. And it was so brave [Teresa], for you to say that. And I agree with you." As Teresa recalls, "I was like 'So why didn't you say so? Why am I the only one who's being forced to confront marketing and telling them that this is a bad idea.'"

In follow-up meetings with several key stakeholders, Teresa became exasperated. As she says,

> I was like, "Yes, but you sent me out there to do research. I went and I did research, I talked to our target market, they're not going to buy this. If we invest in this, we're sinking money. It's like, lost money, basically."

Despite her objections, they moved forward with developing the product. Teresa agreed she'd work just as hard for the product's success despite her objections.

For Teresa this was a "sobering experience." As she says, "We brought all that evidence back. And it was almost like the evidence didn't matter, because they had in their mind made up that we're going to make this product." She says,

> It did make me question, what is it about people? When you show them evidence that this is really not a good idea, we need to pull the plug on this project and do something else, it's almost like they double down on the evidence that they're right.

Teresa mentions she had a "brand" of being "honest about things." In the past, she was always candid about timelines and budgets and was a "very transparent person." She thought her prior relationships and reputation for candor might help her case, but it didn't. Her reputation and evidence didn't help "when people have it in their minds we are doing this project come hell or high water." As Teresa states,

> no amount of evidence is going to change their mind. No amount of advice giving from external people is going to change their mind. Only later on when the evidence kept getting stacked up against this product, did they finally relent.

The project was eventually stopped, but it was many miles down the road and based on a manufacturing issue. Teresa dissented early in the process and could have saved many hundreds of hours and large amounts of money. The larger lessons from Teresa's story are the experience of having solid evidence but not being listened to, as well as confronting powerful interests without the support of others. It's tempting to conclude, from Teresa's experience as well as countless examples, that people aren't persuaded by evidence, but that would be too sweeping a claim that would also ignore numerous counterexamples. Minds do change, but in some circumstances, it is a slow process of accumulating evidence. You may be alone on an island, as Teresa was, but you have a choice: conform or share what you think. Teresa had built up relationships with many of the key decision makers and was a transparent person. Nevertheless, Teresa's experience was "sobering" and, unfortunately, more common than it should be.

We can also see in Teresa's story an honorable integrity to what she saw and the conclusions she reached. Perhaps she was too confident, but she had more first-hand knowledge of the market than the others in the room, yet she was not the ultimate authority and decision maker. Her willingness to speak up was also based on her commitment to the organization. She *cared* whether the organization spent time and money pursuing the product. All of this led to her understandable exasperation.

Nevertheless, she wasn't persuasive and even with the best techniques might have had no luck, but are there effective ways to persuade people with evidence? One method to do so is from the field of motivational interviewing. Motivational interviewing has been used as a method to help individuals rethink deep-seated beliefs, such as a willingness to be vaccinated.[17] It aims to help individuals draw their own conclusions by reflective questions. In doing so, motivational interviewing tries to promote reflective "change talk" as opposed to "sustain talk" (i.e., preserving the status quo). For example, Teresa might have asked, "What needs to be true for this product to be a success?" Or, "If we added benefits to the product, what might they be?" The questions are meant to spark constructive dialogue from individuals with a firm point of view. They don't guarantee success, of course, but, as an approach, it can help avoid arguments where each side digs into their position.

Motivational interviewing is primarily used as a conversational stance when helping individuals in one-on-one sessions. As a method, it aims to explore ambivalence that we both want and don't want change. And to reflectively explore why we *want* change. Rather than trying to persuade anyone, motivational interviewing aims to have individuals persuade themselves. In motivational interviewing, there is effort to respect the autonomy of the individual and, with this, an avoidance of declarative statements that evoke defensiveness and reactance. In this manner, you outline the evidence as you see it and let others make conclusions for themselves. If declarative statements are made where individuals feel forced to "accept the evidence," it can backfire, in the sense that they defensively marshal responses to strengthen their prior position. In Teresa's case, she might have reflected questions from individuals who were considering a different course of action with the product. This might have been done through reflective questioning, such as: what benefits might we potentially add to the product? Or, is there a way to address the issues that these consumers mention?

Likewise, she might have outlined the evidence as clearly as possible from her trip in a way that would help other individuals in the room draw the conclusions that she reached. In this manner, she might have stated, "here's what I saw," or "here's what people said." As one of the leading thinkers on organizational change, John Kotter argues, "The flow of see-feel-change is more powerful than that of analysis-think-change."[18] By this, he means persuasion is easier, in many contexts, by evoking emotions through images and stories. Teresa might have shown pictures or shared stories of her research trip in a way that evoked similar feelings and doubts of the desirability of the product. She would have avoided making declarative statements and asked reflective questions where there was ambivalence and openness. None of this guarantees success, but it can avoid putting people on the defensive that tends to be counterproductive.

Message Medium

In addition to directness and effectively presenting evidence is the tactical consideration of the medium of your message, in particular whether you make your case in writing or in conversation. While the two forms of communication are not mutually exclusive, they have different benefits and drawbacks. This consideration was on the mind of one interviewee named Grace who is a VP of Human Resources at a technology company in California. During the beginning of the COVID-19 pandemic in March 2020, she was following key thought leaders about the future risks associated with the virus and thought her company should move to a work from home policy. The other senior leaders in the company, despite her best efforts at being "data driven" in her arguments, did not want to make the shift. As Grace states, "It was really interesting experience in that regard because I kept trying to have like very logical, rational, measured conversations even though it was an emotional topic for me. And people are just like Yeah, no…just…no."

As Grace states, she thought she could produce "a very logically sound and methodical argument" if she had done it in writing, but she felt it was "an emotional decision." As she states, "do you care about other people getting sick? Yes or no? And the medium for influence seemed like it would be higher if it was a face-to-face conversation with a human rather than reading an e-mail potentially." Accordingly, research has found that messages conveyed through hearing someone's voice are more humanizing and thus more persuasive.[19] Spoken appeals convey the intonations in someone's voice and are harder to dismiss.

Grace also mentioned an awareness of the permanence of making her case in writing. In contrast, conversations are more "ephemeral," which can help mitigate the risk of advocating for controversial viewpoints. As she states:

> I think if you maybe are someone who prefers to write things down or send e-mails or kind of collect your thoughts in writing, there's something so much more permanent about writing. Whereas in a conversation if you're feeling uncomfortable, you can see like social cues. And also nobody knows, nobody really can remember with any sort of credibility, word for word of what you may have said in a conversation and they just feel so much more ephemeral. Whereas, when you write something down, especially nowadays in Slack or e-mail, it's there forever. People can always go back and refer to it and it's in the annals of time, so to speak.

Here, we see—in an analogous fashion to direct speech—how "putting it in writing" can be a risky proposition. It decreases the plausible deniability of your viewpoint (should you be wrong). Thus, "putting it in writing," much like direct speech, can lead to potential reprisal if your proposition is threatening. It signals to those in authority how serious you are. It may be that you want to signal this, but it is a hazard. In contrast, if we make the case in conversation, we can use "trial balloons" or questions that can help us learn about the pushback we'll receive.

On the other hand, you can compose your thoughts more carefully in writing and, at its best, this will give people a chance to think through your ideas. Your ideas also have the potential to reach a wider audience in writing, thus increasing the likelihood you'll receive support. Again, while neither medium precludes the other (and is often determined by the affordances of the situation), we may recognize the hazards of either approach and be inclined toward one or the other. Our inclination, undoubtedly, derives from our perception of skill and personality characteristics (e.g., introversion versus extraversion). Nevertheless, we see Grace considering the impact of putting her viewpoint in writing and she considered the issue to be better made in conversation. Table 3.1 outlines the benefits and drawbacks of either approach.

Table 3.1 Benefits and drawbacks of persuasion attempts in conversation or in writing

	In Conversation	**In Writing**
Benefits	– Emotional appeals might be better made in conversation – Appeals are more humanizing and harder to dismiss – You can respond to counterarguments – You can use indirect language to test the receptivity to your ideas	– Can allow you to clearly compose your perspective – Able to reach a wider audience
Drawbacks/risks	– Heated exchange can lead to muddled arguments and take you beyond the "impropriety threshold"	– Your arguments and ideas are "memorialized." If you change your mind, they can be used against you – Physical tone and cues are not present, which can lead to misunderstandings

Procedural Considerations in Speaking Up

In addition to the message medium, another important consideration is the procedural route you take. This was the case with Evaline who was in the data science department of an organizational development firm. She thought a proposed feature at the end of an employee survey was a "terrible idea." To Evaline, the feature wasn't the best way to have an impact on employee happiness and well-being (its stated intent), and it seemed like they were just following competitors who had a similar feature. When she originally heard about the idea, she said that "so many alarm bells were just going off for me…but then the fact that the rest of the team didn't react that way made me think that oh, maybe I'm crazy."

Late on a Friday afternoon, Evaline had a meeting with the head of her department and happened to mention her dislike of the new product feature. She hadn't planned to do this, but it happened to come up in the conversation. As Evaline says, "So when I asked him to help us shift the direction, like I didn't realize the power that he has, and the trust that he had in me combined, resulted in a catastrophic, full stop on a feature." Immediately the next Monday morning, it led to several "heated discussions" with the head of product and others. As Evaline says, "I was very surprised by the level of immediate support that my leader showed, and the trust as well. But I was also very uncomfortable by the amount of backlash."

After many heated discussions that week, they eventually agreed that the product feature was a "bad idea." Although the outcome was positive for Evaline, "it's still super awkward for me to look at some of these product team members." Evaline says that

I apologized for the way that I brought [it] up. But the fundamental…I think she, the product manager, probably didn't appreciate, still, the way her main thing that she was pushing for is being shut down by one [data science] team member who escalated to the boss without telling her first.

Evaline was concerned that she made the product manager look "terrible and stupid" and regretted the "fighting" and "yelling" that ensued.

In discussion with a leader in the organization, Evaline apologized for escalating the situation the way she did. The leader responded that "it's not that you escalated. It's just that we had so many opportunities in the past that we missed it." But to Evaline the only opportunity she had to express her concerns was in a large group meeting of 40 people (Evaline was not the data science person staffed on the product development team). As Evaline responded, "honestly, it feels so freakin' uncomfortable to speak in front of like 40 people who are…not people that I know."

Evaline was told that her actions would damage the relationship between data science and product development. She saw this in a four-person meeting she had with the head of product and data science. While the meeting started positive, it led to the head of product saying he wanted to prove them wrong and that it was "not OK" to come in so late in the process and stop the feature. Evaline says she was surprised by the "very raw emotional reaction." Here we see a difficult situation for both sides. For Evaline, it led to a great deal of "yelling" and "fighting" and damaged relationships that she didn't want or foresee. For product development, it was a sense of procedural injustice and upset with how the data science department had stopped their work. In this situation, Evaline could learn, as an individual, that she could speak up sooner and use a different avenue, although she hadn't realized her boss would call a full stop on the feature. At another level, her organization could implement a clearer way to receive input from employees in the deliberation phase of the product feature. This would be some way to ask for objections that wouldn't be in a 40-person meeting. These changes were being developed and, as Evaline says, the experience gave them a chance to rethink what "a successful partnership looks like between the two teams."

Evaline, for her part, says she is

super happy with the outcome. I think we got to the right place. I still don't like what happened leading up to that. Obviously, next time I have something like this that doesn't sound right, doesn't feel right, I would have done something more, more productive.

Evaline says she would speak to the "right stakeholders closest to the decision and execution work first." In particular, she would have spoken to the person representing the data science department on the product team along with that individual's manager to list out her concerns. Evaline says this would have been "slower and more work," but ultimately would have saved all the time to "undo the damage." In the story of Evaline, we see her inadvertently bypassing the "right" stakeholders, which led to an escalation of the issue leading to anger and upset among those responsible for the project. It's a reminder to think through the channels of who to speak up to. You might still reach a roadblock and need to escalate the issue further, but you'll give key stakeholders a chance to make their case. Perhaps they'll convince you or you'll convince them.

Thus, another consideration is aiming to bring your concerns to the "right" stakeholder. Determining the "right" stakeholder is a judgment call based on the particulars of the situation, but it's usually the person closest to the situation with direct authority. You may not be persuasive and can then decide another course of action, but if you bypass the stake-holders, it's likely to evoke anger about procedural unfairness (i.e., going around someone's back).

Using Social Proof

Another important means of persuasion is using social proof. Social proof is how "we determine what is correct by finding out what other people think is correct."[20] It is used by advertisers, for example, by stating "a million copies sold." It is a powerful form of persuasion when we are uncertain and thus look to others for proof. In companies, using social proof can involve illustrating effective organizations that have implemented a change. In some respects, however, social proof is antithetical to independent thinking, because, as defined, independent thinking is about being a "lone voice." But social proof can involve bringing evidence from other groups into your present social domain. In one instance, Emily, who worked at a nonprofit, had learned about companies removing their performance reviews in favor of more continuous feedback. As she recalls:

> I started doing research on it, just independently and came up with a viewpoint that I also agreed that traditional performance reviews were not effective. They were extremely biased. They were backward looking, and so they really just didn't serve the purpose that organizations needed it to serve. And so I started to advocate to change, and [my organization] at the time had a very traditional annual review process.

At a meeting where several nonprofits in the local community met, Emily decided to share her point of view on performance management. She says:

> I remember sitting in a meeting and performance management always came up, every meeting. And I raised my hand and I said, "We're actually thinking or looking into if we wanna get rid of traditional performance reviews." And there was an audible gasp in the room. The people were very shocked by it. And I kind of got

the same reaction when I brought it up to the executive team at [my organization]. They were nervous about it; they didn't know how we would manage performance. Would people just do whatever they wanted?

Emily was in the minority opinion for several years, but to build her case she relied on social proof as a means of persuasion. As she recalls, "The way that I went about it was to continue to collect case studies of companies that have done it and did it successfully and really show that our process is not providing value." In a succinct summary of social proof, Emily says, "I think a lot of companies just want somebody else to do it first before they're willing to do it themselves. So I think just seeing the case studies, for them, was helpful in helping the conversation move along."

Social proof is persuasive especially in organizations that are primarily concerned with maintaining legitimacy to external stakeholders, such as nonprofits and educational institutions.[21] In these industries, performance is hard to measure and relatively ambiguous, making it hard to distinguish yourself purely based on creating a ground-breaking product or service. Instead, organizations want to avoid being a deviant in a way that might open them up to external criticism. With legitimacy a primary concern of senior executives, social proof is especially persuasive in these contexts, particularly if that social proof derives from higher status players in the industry (e.g., "look what Harvard is doing"). Emily seemed to intuitively understand this means of persuasion by building her case through providing prominent examples of others changing their performance management process.

Likewise, a similar story emerged from a human resource executive named Jason who wanted to facilitate an Appreciative Inquiry summit at his organization. Appreciative Inquiry is a school of thought that looks to focus on the positive, what is working, and how a compelling future—informed by a broad cross-section of employees—can be developed.[22] Jason had helped the senior management team turn around a failing business in a manufacturing context in around nine months. As Jason said to the senior team, "the last nine months has been focused on what's wrong, what's broken, and fixing it, we need to start shifting the story…around what's working and then growth and prosperity." Jason was learning about Appreciative Inquiry and thought it would be helpful in his current context. Understandably, there was skepticism about his proposal, especially in an organization that revolved around engineering, operations, and finance. As Jason recalls the pushback he received:

> This sounds really touchy feely. You want to bring people in and you want to bring in people from the floor? The forklift drivers and machine operators? They don't really know what's going on. They know their job, but they don't know how to run a business, they don't know how to put a strategy in place. You want to bring them all together and have all these people at the table and talk about what's great about the company and what's working, well, that's not going to work. That won't get us anywhere, because we need to focus on the problems, and what's broken.

Jason persisted, however, and given he had a good relationship with management because he had been a part of the turnaround for the previous nine months, they were more open to listening to his point of view. He said,

> Listen guys, I know what you're saying, and I understand your point of view, but I think this is where we need to go next. If we keep focusing on what's broken, we're not going to grow the business. You want to grow it 10 percent year-over-year for the next three years. This is a company that's lost money for the last two years. We need to do something different.

After some debate, they agreed to think about it further if he could bring some examples of companies that used this "crazy methodology." As Jason recalls,

> That was the learning for me…I should've done that the first time, because what I was presenting was more the methodology and the idea. What I should've done was gone and done some research and found some examples. So I did.

Here, we see again social proof as a powerful means of persuasion. Similar to Emily's story of gathering case studies, Jason went and found similar organizations that had used Appreciative Inquiry. Compared to Emily, it wasn't immediately intuitive for Jason to use social proof as a means of persuasion, but he learned through the process that social proof would be helpful in making his case. Importantly, social proof works the best, of course, if it is similar others, so he had to find companies that were manufacturing and operationally focused. Jason did find several companies and presented the evidence to the senior team. Given this social proof, they decided to have an Appreciative Inquiry summit to help explore how to grow the business. Jason put together a plan for the summit where 10 percent of the company (~100 people), with representative at all levels, were brought in for two days to develop a growth plan. Jason recalls fondly the experience of the summit. As he states:

> It was two days, it was really well received, got great reviews. Some people were crying. These were people like forklift drivers and machine operators, [who] said, "Nobody's ever asked me for my opinion before." There were a couple people who had never been on a plane in their life....We had a guy, an operator, having a conversation with our CFO because a lot of this Appreciative Inquiry summit, there's a lot of people who come together in pairs and they discuss things and then they break out of the groups, etc. That was so successful that we then did another summit to bring in another hundred folks.

Was the summit ultimately successful? The business did grow—based on many factors such as product changes and shifts in marketing strategy. Given the complexity, it would be impossible to pinpoint causality, but the summit helped to shift the attitude. As Jason states, "I think what helped is it helped change the tone, if you will, and the attitude, if that's the right word, or the feeling in the organization that, okay, we're not in trouble anymore, let's think about growth."

Jason recalls how using social proof was critical for being persuasive:

I think the defining moment is being able to bring real-life examples of where other companies used it and it worked. If I wasn't able to come back after that first meeting with some real-life examples, the project never would've happened. At that point, it was just conceptual. That was one of the key learnings that I, even to this day, I always try to incorporate, whenever I'm making a proposal or pitch, is to…take it out of the conceptual and make it real life, what are some of the examples I can give to these leaders?

In Jason's story, we see an inspiring application of Appreciative Inquiry. And to be persuasive, he had to provide social proof from similar organizations.

Credibility and Framing Issues

A final consideration to include in your approach is to link your initiative to important goals and values of the organization. By doing this, you can create tension in decision makers wanting to remain consistent with prior goals and values.[23] This tactic often links an idea to an important value or aspiration and can simply be framed, "If we value x, then…" or "If we are trying to be the top provider of Y, then…" This strategy is fairly intuitive, but it takes effort to make the issue less about *you* and more about the organization. For example, Carmen Medina, a former employee at the CIA and coauthor of *Rebels at Work*, mentions she had many ideas to improve the agency early in her career.[24] She hadn't built her status and credibility, however, and her ideas were dismissed. After proving her competence over many years in several roles, she began to establish her credibility and shift the way she was framing issues. As she says:

So instead of standing on the soapbox and saying, "We have to be completely different, or we're going to die!" you know, which is what I did in the late '90s, I think you need to say, "The organization has this objective, and I think these ideas could help us achieve these objectives more effectively." And I think you need to start there.[25]

You can see how this calmer approach helps and how being an alarmist, without status or credibility, is unlikely to be effective. In the study of persuasion, there are two main factors that establish credibility: expertise and trustworthiness.[26] Both of these factors take time to build throughout one's career. It may require strategic patience before advocating for big ideas until you've built credibility. However, even if you have lower credibility, there is the hopeful phenomenon known as the "sleeper effect." The "sleeper effect" occurs when the strength of the argument, over time, becomes more important than the message source.[27] People begin to forget who advocated for an idea; they just mull over of the idea, itself. This can work in your favor if you haven't established your credibility but your idea has merit. This was illustrated in a large-scale research study in the health care sector where ideas were tracked over 31 months. Researchers found that among 208 voiced ideas, the vast majority were immediately dismissed. However, 49 eventually reached implementation, often through another person, a process the researchers call "voice cultivation."[28] Voice cultivation commonly occurred through allyship where ideas became legitimized over time when others advocated for them. This highlights that while you may not have credibility in the moment, ideas can eventually gain traction.

In addition to your credibility, you also have to make a compelling case that it will be valuable to the organization, as obvious as that might seem. One individual I spoke to named Matt was an officer in the U.S. Army and was not successful in his influence attempt. Matt wanted to change the evaluation system for the personnel of an Army training school he was overseeing. His direct reports in the training school were evaluated by a commanding officer who had limited contact with these individuals, and they were routinely not given the highest ratings. As in many large corporations, the Army only had so many top evaluations that could be given (there was a forced distribution), and the individuals in the training school weren't receiving these top evaluations, no matter how well they did. There was a matrix structure to the organization, however; so Matt thought the evaluation ratings should be completed by another department that had more interaction with the training school and could render more accurate and fair judgments. Matt was motivated by a "strong belief that the system was unfair."

Matt discussed changing the system with the Chief of Staff of the other department—a department he thought could render a fairer evaluation of the lieutenants. However, he met immediate resistance and was told he needed more "data," although he had no access to that data. As Matt says:

> I think a lot of things that you speak up about…many times, it's just putting more work on someone else's plate, or it's like another thing that somebody has to worry about. In getting, somehow getting their buy in as to why doing that extra amount of work was valuable to the organization.

There is a natural resistance to new ideas that need a threshold level of excitement. You need to overcome the reality that the idea will cause disruption and effort to implement, and while the situation may exhibit an injustice or unfairness to you, it needs to be framed in a way that makes this salient to your audience. You want to frame the current practice as contradicting an organization's values and goals. The inconsistency between an espoused value and a current practice can be a powerful argument for change.

Matt was not able to change the evaluation system, but upon reflection he says he would have done two things differently. First, he would have "assumed positive intent" upon the part of the commanding officer who was completing the evaluations. He might have discussed with the commanding officer his ratings decisions to see if he could gently ask him to reconsider or explore the reasoning for the ratings. While unlikely to be successful, Matt would have more "data" and experience in trying to change the system *within* the system, rather than assuming ill-intent. Second, he would have reframed the argument to be about "driving people out of the Army." As he says:

> We're bringing these people over where they are at a critical point where they're deciding whether or not they stay in the Army. And this is just an experience that's driving people out of the Army, to be quite honest, because they're like, "well, I got selected for this position. And then was essentially just given a bad evaluation because of the system wasn't created or aligned properly."

Here, we see how trying to reframe the issue as of central importance to the organization might have been more persuasive. It moved the issue from "this is unfair to these individuals" to "this isn't helping our organization meet its long-term goals." So, an important consideration in persuasiveness is both establishing your credibility and then framing your issue in a way that demonstrates an inconsistency with the values and aspirations of the organization. While the issue might be of personal importance, linking it to *shared* goals improves your chance of success.

Summary

Throughout this chapter, we saw many ways to be more persuasive in situations where you do not have formal authority and cannot mandate compliance. During the process of persuasion, we first need to keep our anger from crossing the "impropriety threshold" to the point where our conduct becomes the focus of attention and not our ideas. Anger, as a cue to a violated value, is often a motivator behind our actions, but we need to "rock the boat but keep it steady."

To effectively persuade, we looked at several considerations, including:

1. Asking questions versus being direct
2. Effectively presenting evidence in a way that helps others see what you see
3. Choosing your message medium, whether it is in conversation or in writing
4. Procedural considerations of engaging stakeholders who are directly involved with an issue
5. Using social proof for the value of your idea
6. Establishing your credibility and framing issues in alignment with organizational values and goals

Now that we've explored specific tactics to improve your persuasiveness, let's look at the process of leading change over time.

CHAPTER 4

Leading Change

While the previous chapter looked at persuasion tactics and considerations, this chapter will broaden the scope to explore the process of leading change when you have limited formal authority (i.e., you are not a CEO). If you are immediately successful in getting a green light on your idea, what should you do next? And if you don't get a green light, in some circumstances, do you proceed anyway? And what are some models and mindsets to help you implement change? These are the questions this chapter explores. Let's first look at implementing change after you receive an endorsement of your idea.

Speaking Up and Then Implementing Change

As any successful entrepreneur would say, having a good idea is not enough; you need to be able to implement it. This was the case for Will who had a plan to redesign the training approach of his large, multinational technology company. Will had worked at the company for many years when his department got a new boss who oversaw both technical and sales training. Will saw many inefficiencies in the department and developed a plan to redesign their work. He brought up his plans with his new boss late in a meeting and his boss said to outline his plans in a proposal the next day. He worked with a colleague late that evening to prepare a presentation. She agreed with the major points, and Will remembers her saying, "This is pretty radical," and this might be a "CLM—a career limiting maneuver."

Will was fine with taking the risk as he was considering other job opportunities. So he gave the presentation remotely via audio and screen share (before video conferencing was readily available). As Will recalls, "I say here, listen, here's what we need to do. I developed this whole structure of content." Instead of a "hodgepodge of classes," Will outlined

100-, 200-, 300-, 400-, and 500-level classes. If you already knew the 100 level, then you could start at the 200-level class. As he says:

> It was gonna pretty radically change things because we'd have to have a consistency from the technical trainers to the sales trainers. And the technical trainers didn't really think the sales trainers were any good…It would solve a bunch of our problems and we can hit different audiences with different sets of content…I said, "what we're doing is wrong. Or, you know, just not very efficient."

Will recalls how he didn't have any video or verbal feedback through most of the presentation and he was worried he had committed a "career limiting maneuver." After a pause, his boss responded, "What you just said here is what I want our entire department to do. Everyone under me, we're gonna go in your direction, I want you to lead it." In the world of status quo bias and vested interests, this is as good as speaking up can go. Will was promoted in three months and received a huge bonus that year.

Although Will was able to get his boss on board, the difficulty was in implementing the new structure and leading this change. As Will recalls, the technical trainers "found out fairly quickly, they could just keep doing the same thing they were doing." "They kept doing things, the old way, they just resisted change. They fought every way, every which way about it." "The whole thing eventually failed." His boss moved on. Will said he lost his patience and had enough of "the big company environment" and moved to a different organization.

Any failure is multifaceted, but Will came to the conclusion that "This isn't a problem of whether I have the right thing. It's a problem of change. This is an organizational change problem. People are not willing to change." Will says he needed more authority and better project management skills with a status board of when people would complete different tasks. He also says his boss was "too much of a big picture guy" and wasn't authoritative in saying "we're not doing it the old way."

Thus, while I have stressed independent thinking and speaking up about original ideas to those in senior positions, that is only part of the story. Persuading others in the organization is also central to implementing your idea. Although the change was persuasively outlined to his boss, others failed to see its inherent advantages. One person's innovative solution is another person's painstaking change. It's hard to get collective agreement on a common problem (as discussed in the first chapter), especially when there is not an objective standard to draw from, such as investment returns. For Will, there were inefficiencies and training that was not designed for specific audiences. To him, this was a problem, and in leading the change he didn't have enough authority to force compliance.

The leadership scholar Ron Heifetz describes the process of leading without formal authority.[1] This means you do not have power, based on your position, to mandate compliance. Mandating compliance is efficient, of course, but it can backfire. Softer tactics are needed, such as acknowledging the loss people will experience. As Heifetz states, people need to

> see that you understand the loss you are asking them to accept. You need to name the loss, be it a change in time-honored work routines or an overhaul of the company's core values, and explicitly acknowledge the resulting pain.[2]

As Will had more distance from the failure, he realized acknowledging loss was one thing he failed to do. He says, "they have to kind of say goodbye to the old thing." This might be done in a symbolic way, as Will recalled a story of an airline that merged and gave employees toys with the old airline name on it.

Will also wondered if he immediately put people on the defensive by framing the redesign as if they were currently "wrong" in how they did their work. This was a winning argument with his boss, but with others, their response was, "you're telling us we're doing this wrong." Will says he had to "really backtrack" after several meetings and tell them that "it's not that you guys are not working hard. It's just that we're not working efficiently." Defensiveness and thus resistance to change can happen for many reasons, including our sense of competence being threatened, time-honored routines being discarded, or a sense that our freedom and autonomy are being taken from us.

In most accounts of leading change effectively, involving others to gain buy-in is central. Involvement can dampen the sense that things are happening *to* us without our input. In some situations, we may not be resisting the content of change, but the way it's communicated to us. We are reacting negatively to being controlled or having our autonomy threatened. This has been found in research on jurors who were either told evidence was inadmissible or given a long-winded and condescending explanation for why they couldn't consider the evidence. The researchers found that when jurors were given the condescending explanation, they reacted by still considering the evidence compared to the more neutral explanation.[3] In psychology, this is called "psychological reactance," which is an aversion to our freedom being taken away and a dislike of being controlled.[4] By involving others in the process of change, we can partly mitigate reactance.

One mindset that helps you take action and involve others is confident humility.[5] It is to be confident in yourself but humble that you could be wrong or at least aware that you don't have all the answers. It is a balancing act of being confident enough to take action, but humble and open to how you can change course.[6] When you are excessively certain (confident with little humility), it can provoke defensiveness in others as we saw in Will's case.

Will also says, "We needed heroes, who were the people that actually made this change." In essence, he needed greater involvement from others in leading the change. In a comprehensive review of the link between effective leadership and change, the key attributes that promoted success were effective communication, being supportive of the concerns of change recipients, and involving followers.[7] By Will's own account, he missed on all three facets. He communicated the change in a way that made recipients defensive, as if everything they had been doing was wrong. He also didn't acknowledge the loss recipients would experience as they had to give up favored routines and classes they had taught. Finally, he didn't work to effectively involve others, perhaps by highlighting "heroes" that were making the change.

Ultimately, Will wasn't able to implement the change. But, as is often the case, failure is an effective, yet unwelcome teacher. As he says, "I thought I learned more from that failure than from many other things in my career." Will learned he needed a comprehensive set of tactics to lead change. It wasn't enough to win over his boss with the logic of his ideas; he needed to get others onboard. Thus, we need to be able to effectively speak up about our innovative ideas, but also lead others through the process of implementing those ideas.

The importance of change management was also evident for Amy, who was staffed as the "change" person on a digital transformation team. As she says:

> When I first joined digital transformation, the belief was that they were going to build products—they're going to be so human centered that everyone would love them and just use them. And I had to work really, really hard to challenge that notion that, "No, you are not Steve Jobs, and you are releasing products into a workplace that changes people's daily work." Totally different type of adoption than putting something into the App Store.

When Amy began, the team's "level of belief in change" was a "one" on a scale of 1 to 10 (with one being the lowest). Two leaders on the team were the biggest skeptics for having "change at the table." They "did not believe that it was an issue in any way, shape, or form." The biggest assumption she needed to challenge was that "once the tool is done, you just launch it. And that's it. There's no other work that needs to be done." For Amy, speaking up was about the idea of change management itself, for its importance in helping the team and organization meet its goals.

The skepticism to change management is common and multifaceted. Paul Gibbons, author of *The Science of Successful Organizational Change*, describes how advocacy for change management is often unwelcome. He says:

> Change experts can be wet blankets. We make projects more socially complex, raise stakeholder risks, recommend involvement (usually), challenge cultural norms, and require resources and senior leadership time to address those risks. We advocate time-consuming engagement up front: "It is doubtful that engineering will accept that quality control process without extensive involvement in its design."[8]

Similarly, one of the core aspects of Amy's advocacy was getting them to be "empathetic with the idea that individuals move through a change journey...you can't just flick a switch." She wanted employees to feel like they had a "voice in the product" and that there was "engagement from day one." She worked on several avenues, including making sure each product had enough sponsorship throughout the organization and there were metrics of a new product's adoption. She wanted to make sure they "created employee engagement so that employees feel like at least they're represented, or their colleague is at the table to help design these products." In this, you can see how involvement in the process can facilitate success, although it is more time consuming and, of course, can lead to feedback and conversations that are seemingly (and often) unproductive. Nevertheless, when you can't mandate compliance, it is important that individuals feel like they are being respected and involved. There are instances where compliance is mandated, as Amy says, there were some initiatives "where if you want to be an employee here, you have to take part in this change." In others, however, you build support through involvement.

Amy also advocated for understanding how the technology adoption curve could help the team by "identifying your early adopters and innovators and helping to use them to create momentum." The technology adoption curve is a categorization of when individuals adopt a new technology. It is illustrated as a bell curve with the first 2.5 percent of adopters called "innovators" and the next 13.5 percent called "early adopters." They are followed by the "early majority, late majority, and laggards."[9] The model helps you segment individuals and attunes you to find the innovators and early adopters to build momentum and social proof for your initiative.

Everett Rodgers, who outlined the technology adoption curve in his book *Diffusion of Innovations,* describes several ways to find the "opinion leaders" among innovators and early adopters. Opinion leaders, based on their influential position in the informal network, can help spread ideas and innovations. Ways of finding opinion leaders include asking key informants who these people are, or, in an employee survey, asking: "Who are the three (or four or five) other individuals with whom you would discuss adopting this innovation?" In an employee survey, you can also ask individuals to self-designate by asking "Do you think people come to you for information or advice more often than to others?"[10]

In addition to guiding you to find opinion leaders among early adopters, the technology adoption curve normalizes resistance. If approximately 16 percent of people (give or take) are going to be venturesome "early adopters," then 84 percent of people are going to initially resist. Rather than viewing this group as resistors, you can view their reluctance as a valuable source of information. There may be ways to improve your product, ideas, or initiative based on the feedback from these groups, rather than viewing their resistance as purely a form of recalcitrance.[11] In some circumstances, individuals directly involved in a process may have better knowledge of the benefits of a current system and how it can be improved. This view of resistance can promote a virtuous cycle of learning and improving your ideas.

In understanding adoption as a gradually increasing curve, it also helps you see that you need a "critical mass" or "tipping point," where diffusion is slow until it accelerates.[12] This realization helps justify efforts to promote the change in its early stages to help its future success. At the same time, however, the technology adoption curve is not a preordained path for every new initiative. When considering voluntary adoption, the desirability and relative advantage of the new initiative needs to be sufficiently high to change a person's routines. In organizations, a large percentage of changes are made by those in a position of authority and are not optional. In these cases, the change process is more about effective training, implementation, and speed of transition that mitigates short-term performance setbacks. Change management in these circumstances is focused on effective communication to reduce levels of uncertainty, confusion, and stress.

Table 4.1 outlines the two different forms of change—mandated or voluntary—and tactics associated with each.

In leading change efforts, we also need (and are aided by) social support. Although Amy was staffed on the digital transformation team as her full-time role, she did have a boss who was setting up a change center of excellence in the company that gave her support. Her boss would come over from time to time so "she had my back." However, for Amy "it was me fighting a lot." She also began to receive peer support on the digital

Table 4.1 Types of change and corresponding change tactics

Type of Change	Key Considerations	Example Change Tactics
Top-down change (mandated)	Managing stress on system to mitigate short-term performance setbacks and overwhelming employees	– Communicate clear timelines to reduce uncertainty, offer training, and so on – Approach the situation with empathy by acknowledging loss and offering reassurance as way to manage stress/uncertainty
Initiative led by change agent without formal authority (voluntary adoption)	"Softer tactics" needed to promote adoption of idea/product by persuading individuals of its relative advantage	– Establish your credibility and reputation (i.e., informal authority) as a change agent – Persuade opinion leaders, key sponsors, and potential early adopters – With empathy, acknowledge loss but appeal to relative advantage of change – Build a guiding coalition to provide advice and social support – Avoid "psychological reactance" to change by promoting involvement – Use soft methods of accountability (e.g., project boards/documents with names of volunteers) – Demonstrate early "small wins" with pilots/prototypes

transformation team, including another staff hire, so that she wasn't on a "crusade" by herself. This highlights one of the central components of leading change, which is to build a "guiding coalition."[13] John Kotter, one of the leading thinkers on organizational change, recommends having employees complete applications to be on the guiding coalition and says they should be comprised of individuals from a wide-variety of levels in the organization.[14] For Amy, it wasn't a formalized process, but she was building social support in a similar manner.

Over time, the digital transformation team began to see the difficulty of not dedicating time to change. As Amy says, they were often

> feeling the pain of if you don't do adoption well, you have a mess on your hands, and you just can't deliver on the value that you need. I mean we have shut down products, literally shut down products that didn't have adoption.

Given the failed rates of change (often reported at 70 percent of initia-tives),[15] the process is often handled poorly. For Amy, she says that given all her work over three years, she was able to move her skeptics to a 10 on a 1 to 10 scale on their belief in change. One of the two biggest skeptics even wrote a note that said, "[Amy] removed the scales from my eyes, and taught me the value of change, people's change journey, the tech adoption curve." And he said, "Now I see every problem as a change problem."

Even though you may have good ideas, *how* you implement them is equally important. We see in Will's case a good idea that was resisted given there was limited involvement in its conception and potential adoption. It wasn't a mandated change and Will needed a more comprehensive set of tactics to get everyone involved. For Amy, she was advocating for the very idea of change management itself. As a set of considerations, change management can lengthen the process of implementation. But, as Amy's skeptics eventually discovered, without consideration for the change process, many ideas and initiatives won't make it very far.

Asking Forgiveness, Rather Than Permission

In leading change, you can also fail to get the immediate endorsement of your idea from senior leaders because you haven't created a strong enough case for change (at least from their perspective). One reason you won't be persuasive is that you cannot demonstrate, conclusively with evidence, that you will be successful. This is especially true if you are on the edge of new and innovative ideas, and thus by definition, you won't have much evidence in support of your idea. It's hard to be persuasive without evi-dence of the results you can create until you can create them. This was evident in several interviews where good ideas were stifled, but individu-als decided to move forward regardless. This is the commonly used tactic of asking for forgiveness rather than permission.

In one interview I conducted, Maya told her story of implementing her vision, despite being told to stick with the company's approach. Maya was named regional president for a Southeast Asian advertising company. She was brought in to spur growth because results had been lagging in the region. As part of her approach, she wanted to create an inspiring vision to raise the bar for performance. Although the company had a global vision, to Maya it was the "lowest common denominator" because it was meant to be applicable in over 80 countries. Maya had tried to use the company vision to inspire employees, but it wasn't working, so she decided to create something on her own. For Maya, the central aspect of her vision was to ask if any idea or proposal was *unimaginable*. She wanted a simple word and visual imagery that employees "could actually go to sleep and wake up with." As Maya says,

> I wanted something that could thread through everything, which would be simple to remember. And it would be very black-and-white, like, is it this or not? And I was reading a poem. And that word, I just picked it up from a poem.

She shared this idea with her boss as part of her growth strategy, but he rejected the idea. He said, "We already have a vision…You cannot go off and create another one." Maya shared how she'd been struggling to spur growth and how she needed to "try something different." She even shared how she wanted to visualize her new approach to inspire growth. However, her boss insisted that there was a global company vision and she should stick with that. When asked how she left the meeting, Maya says:

> I knew I wanted to do this. But I wasn't going to sit and have another two-hour discussion with him and try to convince him of what I was doing. So that's when I was like, I don't have to tell him a yes or no right now. I'm very convinced what I'm doing is right, my team kind of thinks it's the right thing. So we're gonna go ahead and do it. And then we will see what comes out of it.

As Maya describes her decision,

> I decided just to not ask for permission anymore. And just go ahead and do it. And if it worked, I knew he would be fine with it. And if it didn't, I would get screwed, but I would have got screwed in any case, if we hadn't grown, right? So I thought there was just no point in asking for permission.

At the heart of Maya's vision was that "everything had to be unimaginable. If it wasn't, then sorry, it had to be scrapped." The word was a simple test meant to "raise the bar." For any idea: "Was it unimaginable? Or was it so ordinary that it wasn't unimaginable, right?" As Maya states,

> If we have to grow from zero to 300, everything we have to do has to be unimaginable…Every person that we hire has to be with that lens…When we are servicing clients, the service has to be something which is unimaginable. The tools we are creating or inventing, that has to be unimaginable.

If an employee came to her, "I would ask them. Do you think this is unimaginable? And like, no, it isn't? Okay, well, out it goes."

Maya didn't want to force her interpretation of what unimaginable meant, either. She wanted to get employees to own it for themselves and build on what inspired them. As she said to her direct reports: "This is the transformation I'm looking for. Now, for each country CEO, what does it mean for you and your team? Come back and tell me."

With this new focus and simple test of everything they were doing, they began to see changes within six months, including bringing in new business and improved client evaluation scores. The vision was "really transformational for the region." They achieved growth beyond the metrics they had set and "turned around the corner in every which way."

Maya continued to keep it quiet from her boss for close to a year before he heard that "Asia was running their own thing." When Maya had her year-end evaluation, she was given some "grief" for "wanting to do her own thing," but since she had the results it was forgiven. Her boss, however, didn't want to acquiesce and responded that "we've got our global vision, let's just stick with that."

In Maya's story, we see the process of leading change through inspiring employees to move beyond the ordinary. She wasn't content with "following orders" and had an inspiring message to spur growth. She had a conviction that this approach would work, and it was authentic to her. It illustrates that, in some situations, even if you don't get a green light, it's worth pursuing your course of action. At the same time, it's hard to

see what is objectionable with her approach. Why stop her from raising standards with the language she was using? Her supervisor's lack of
approval hints at the hierarchy of control in most organizations and how
leading change can quickly impinge upon this control structure. Maya's
framing of the situation as creating her own vision was threatening, much
like saying, "I have my own strategy for the organization." There is a
balance that needs to occur between top-down execution and bottom-up
innovation and change. If you are leading change from the bottom (or
mid-level), you'll inevitably face resistance with a desire for control, but
you can frame things in a less threatening way to manage this balance.
For example, Maya might have framed her approach as a way to "improve
performance" rather than a new vision. The important point, in leading
change, is to be aware of the perceptions from above, and manage these
perceptions until you can build your credibility and show results.

In a similar story of moving ahead with an initiative, even after being
told no, was an individual named Kelly, who was in her first marketing position at a retreat center in 2008. At the time, social media was
just starting to increase in popularity, with growth beginning to surge
on Facebook and Twitter. The retreat center would host educational
conferences, and Kelly got to know several forward-thinking advisors of
the retreat center who were developing ways to leverage social media.
However, the executive director wanted to have a very "controlled
message." It was one-way communication where messages were on the
website and catalogs. As Kelly says, "it was all [the retreat center's] voice,
the way they wanted to be perceived."

Kelly began to think about leveraging social media to help the
retreat center, in particular "the importance of the story of the people
who attended versus having that controlled voice." Kelly met with the
executive director to outline why a presence on social media was something they should pursue. In response, however, Kelly says "it was a hard
'no'...it was 'nope, we need to be able to control our message. This is the
way it is'... [the executive director] was very much, 'it's my voice that
is this company.'" Kelly was "really, really disappointed." After thinking
it through, Kelly decided that instead of continuing to "fight the battle," she would go "rogue." She began creating social media accounts and
"testing things out" without the executive director knowing. Kelly began

"building a following" and doing so in a "stealth way." She knew that the executive director wasn't on social media, and over a short period of time, she was able to build up a following of around 500 people.

She decided to have a second meeting with the executive director to present the case for a social media strategy. For Kelly, the worst-case scenario would be to delete all the accounts. Kelly was intentional about the core message she wanted to deliver in the meeting. She didn't want it to seem like she was just being "rebellious" or was just using the technology "because it's the hot new thing." For Kelly, the core of why she believed this was a worthwhile strategy was connected to the purpose of the retreat center which was transformational experiences. As she says,

> the real story, what people need to hear, and what they're going to connect with, are those personal transformation stories…If we really want to take this and elevate the work and really bring it to the next level, we can't just keep ourselves with our one voice, we have to make it so other people are sharing their voices about it.

Kelly wanted to connect with this purpose in framing her argument to the executive director. She also developed a presentation with the numbers and engagement levels and how they could even "control the voice a little bit."

In addition to preparing herself for the meeting, Kelly spoke to several advisors of the retreat center about her initiative, including individuals who had developed expertise in social media strategies. They agreed that they'd be happy to answer any additional questions from the executive director that Kelly couldn't answer. In the meeting itself, Kelly presented her case, showed what she'd been doing, and answered questions about how much time it took to manage. Near the end, she mentioned that she spoke with several of the advisors and that "they're on board" and "can help support it." This is where the executive director "got the most mad," that Kelly had "gotten them on board without her permission…It wasn't that I had gone and created the social media accounts but was actually in creating some allies within our supporters in this area." Kelly says at this point she really "shut down" and that it was "brutal." She says she was "ready to call it quits" but had made a big commitment in relocating for this job. Eventually, however, the executive director's "viewpoint changed," in part based on conversation with advisors.

Kelly wasn't happy with the experience and wonders what she might have done differently; perhaps she might have had the advisors make the case to the executive director rather than herself. She did continue in her role for several more years and when she left they continued with a social media marketing approach. When asked what motivated her in this situation, Kelly says, "I really respected these advisors…they're smart, smart people. And I didn't want to be the person in that, like in that role where you could make a difference and not, and not do it." Similar to other stories in this book, Kelly was seeing an emerging trend and following advice of forward-thinking advisors. She wasn't inventing this new world, of course, but saw its potential to help further the cause of the retreat center, a cause she believed in.

Similar to Maya's story, Kelly took a professional risk. They both had innovative ideas for improving their organizations but needed to begin implementing those ideas to prove their worth. This motivation was combined with being dutiful and asking for permission. However, their ideas didn't conform with current practices or were considered too risky. Thus, they found themselves in the position of being passionate about their ideas, but to follow through on them, they needed to disobey authority. They took a calculated risk in being proactive, to demonstrate their ideas with tangible results. This leads to a tempered conclusion, similar to many we've explored: In several situations, being an independent thinker will put you on the edge of what is proven. To implement your idea, you'll need to take a calculated risk (and then ask for forgiveness).

Phases of Change

Given these stories of leading change, let's look at a generalized model of planned change. Planned change contrasts with the continuous, everyday change we all experience. It connotes intentionally improving an organization over time. In synthesizing across published models, I outline three phases or best practices of change.[16] As mentioned previously, the emphasis in this chapter is leading change with little formal authority (i.e., you can't mandate compliance given your positional power). These three phases/best practices are:

1. Engage in discovery. (Generate insights and develop empathy.)
2. Make a compelling case for change. (Create dissatisfaction with status quo.)
3. Take an experimental mindset. (Aim for small wins/losses to promote learning.)

Engaging in planned change should begin with discovery. Discovery incorporates a wide range of research activities, including interviewing stakeholders, collecting survey data about opinions and attitudes, and exploring best practices and market trends. The point of discovery is that while you may have hunches that you know the biggest challenges, your perspective is likely to be *partially* informed. However, you are unlikely to realize the limits of your knowledge. As mentioned in Chapter 2, the Nobel Prize winning psychologist Daniel Kahneman, who pioneered research on cognitive biases, states, "The remarkable aspect of our mental life is that we are rarely stumped."[17] We can develop strong opinions of what needs to change based on little information, although it is difficult to realize this. Thus, the mental challenge that must be overcome to engage in discovery is certainty and overconfidence. It requires a degree of intellectual humility, of knowing you don't know.[18] By engaging in discovery, we begin to realize the limits of our knowledge.

Throughout the process, the aim is to explore the wants, needs, and perspectives of stakeholders with an open mind. While discovery can validate assumptions about what needs to change, it will inform you of many things you didn't realize. Discovery adds time to the equation, however, and everything has opportunity costs. Nevertheless, before trying to change any system you need to understand it first. And engaging in discovery is an investment of time that increases your chances of success for the future. This makes discovery as close to a "golden rule" as possible.

Central to the process of discovery is speaking with people who will be impacted by or responsible for any potential change. When interviewing potential "end users" about the current system and processes, it helps to gather detailed stories of specific actions, when applicable.[19] Asking for specific stories of individuals can help overcome the limits of self-knowledge. Individuals may be introspective and aware of their motivations, but we don't have complete self-knowledge. In some situations, there is a gap between what we say and what we do. By asking for tangible actions and experiences, we can mitigate the gap between a person's theory of behavior from one's actual behavior.

This gap can be overstated, of course, but its presence is especially acute when there is social desirability to behavior. In discovery, you want to gather information about what people *actually think,* not what people are supposed to say. Thus, you want to avoid questions that might have a high social desirability bias in their response, such as "What have you done to implement our current strategy?" When interviewing, you want to create a psychologically safe environment that reduces performative answers and impression management. This is complicated if you are doing discovery in your own organization but can be mitigated by assurances of confidentiality and by taking a neutral, open-minded stance as an interviewer. If the change topic is too fraught for in-person interviews, an alternative path is open-ended questions in anonymous surveys.

Another tactic to gather specific stories is to ask for high points and low points. This can help to understand salient events over time. By first asking for high points, you can set a positive tone from which you can learn low points (or pain points). For example, you can first ask, "what are the high points of using our current system?" From this, you can build some initial rapport before exploring low points or pain points. By gathering specific stories of actions, you can draw inferences across individuals from tangible experiences. Ultimately, while time consuming, discovery will help generate insights, develop empathy for those impacted by the change, and help inform your approach.

In addition to generating insights, the process of discovery also begins to socialize your ideas as individuals become aware of a potential change. This learning process can help mitigate change resistance in the future, as individuals have a chance to share their thoughts, opinions, and experiences. This is commonly referred to as "procedural justice," which is the perceived fairness of a process. It is a concept we will return to in the next chapter when considering the importance of creating a fair process for individuals to share their ideas.

While I stress interviewing as a primary mode of discovery, it can include researching best practices in other organizations or conducting an employee survey to explore opinions about an issue. Ultimately, the process of discovery helps establish your credibility and expertise as you make the case for change. It builds the evidence and insights you'll need. It won't just be your opinion, but you can say, "after speaking with x number of employees" or "from surveys responses we reviewed, the biggest issue is x." It will make your case for change more persuasive and informed.

This leads us to the second phase of planned change, which is to make a compelling case for change. This is often described as "unfreezing," "creating a sense of urgency," or inducing "survival anxiety" (i.e., "if we don't change, we're not going to survive").[20] Unsurprisingly, it's difficult to break individuals and organizations out of routines and patterns that have been established. By and large, routines and patterns have been functional, so the change needs to be compelling enough to overcome the status quo. With voluntary change, the *relative advantage* of a new way of working needs to clear, as Everett Rodgers outlined in his seminal book *Diffusion of Innovations.* The challenge, in many cases, is that the relative advantage is clear to us but not others. This may lead us to decry that there is "resistance to change," but if we've done our discovery right, we'll understand and empathize with this resistance. Again, discovery sets the stage for effectively making the case for change (or realizing the change is only compelling to a small number of individuals).

The mental challenge in this phase is overcoming the curse of knowledge. The curse of knowledge occurs when we are highly immersed in a domain such that we take for granted problems and assumptions.[21] It is hard to imagine the mind of a novice or someone not immersed in our domain. We assume everyone has the same knowledge that we do, and therefore skip over discussing the problem and forget to convince others that there *is* a problem. As the organizational psychologist Adam Grant states:

> Before people will believe that your idea will make the world better, you have to explain what's wrong with the world right now...
> In his most famous speech, Martin Luther King, Jr. didn't open with his dream. Before turning to his vision for tomorrow, he

spent the first 11 of his 16 minutes describing the injustice of today. As communication expert Nancy Duarte explains, you have to show people what's unacceptable about "what is" before they'll get excited about "what could be."[22]

This highlights how, in making the case for change, we don't want to forgo describing "what is" before describing "what could be." The gap between these two can spur change, but given the curse of knowledge, we might skip over describing the current problem and move right to our big idea.

Creating tension between "what is" and "what could be" is especially important when an organization is in a stable position. When there is a crisis, however, a sense of urgency and survival anxiety may already be prevalent, making your case for change easier. Individuals will be more open to change when performance is below aspiration levels.[23] A crisis can be too extreme, of course, in a way that can lead to "threat rigidity," where we decrease our processing of information and over-rely on pre-existing responses.[24] Given moderate levels of stability, however, creating tension between "what is" and "what could be" can be utilized to help overcome the status quo.

In addition to adequately describing the problem in a way that creates dissatisfaction with the status quo, many of the persuasion tactics mentioned in the previous chapter are also applicable, including effectively presenting evidence, choosing your message medium, procedural considerations of engaging stakeholders, using social proof, establishing your credibility, and framing issues in alignment with organizational values and goals.

A third phase or best practice in leading change is to take an experimental mindset. Viewing implementation as an "experiment" can lower the stakes. If you are aiming for a "big splash" or to create a "finely polished apple," then the inevitable roadblocks you'll face will be more threatening. They won't be something to learn from and adjust.

One way to take an experimental mindset is to seek "small wins" or to learn from "small losses."[25] Aiming for "small wins" has a tradition in the field of organizational change, often labeled "short-term wins."[26] In the product world, the same logic is often referred to as a "minimal viable product," which helps to overcome delays in launching a product by getting the simplest version released from which you can learn and iterate. A small wins approach helps to build momentum, increase one's sense of efficacy, and provides feedback to learn and improve. As the organizational psychologist Karl Weick states, "Having imposed the logic of small wins on a situation cognitively, the person then wades into the situation and acts with persistence, confidence, and forcefulness."[27] Small wins can also help build your case for change as you can demonstrate some initial success. We saw this in the case of Maya and Kelly who were able to demonstrate some results to bolster their case for change.

If you are aiming for a "small win," if you don't succeed, it will be a "small loss." Small losses are easier to learn from and less damaging to your reputation and credibility. They will certainly sting, but to a lesser degree and the situation can be framed as an "experiment." As Sim Sitkin states in his article "Learning Through Failure: The Strategy of Small Losses," "In the face of large and potentially threatening losses, organizational responses are more likely to be protective than exploratory."[28] Keeping the process of change in the exploratory realm, as opposed to "blame and shame," helps to continue momentum, adjust, and persist.

The mental challenge to overcome in taking an experimental mindset is overoptimism. Being overly optimistic might lead to a large-scale rollout of a change with little awareness of tenuous assumptions. We won't begin to see these tenuous assumptions until we've begun implementing a new process. Think of Will's rollout of a new curriculum earlier in the chapter. If he had taken an experimental mindset to test some of his assumptions on one part of the curriculum, he could have learned about the resistance and complications he would face. Learning about them on a smaller scale is less threatening and, with an experimental mindset, can be productive feedback to alter your ideas.

Although a certain degree of optimism is needed to help us move forward, we are inevitably dealing with partial information and do not have perfect certainty in how the future will unfold. As Cass Sunstein, a lawyer and social scientist who worked in the Obama administration, describes, it helps to have a certain level of "productive anxiety." This is having a healthy concern and skepticism about what might go wrong. This contrasts with being overly optimistic. As he states,

> In the Obama administration, for example, most officials were not complacent, but some of them were; they thought that the Affordable Care Act could be implemented with only a few glitches, that Democrats and Republicans would work together, and that policies would work just as the administration hoped.[29]

While a moderate level of optimism can be beneficial, it helps to have healthy skepticism about how the future will unfold. Taking an experimental mindset to aim for small wins or losses can help with the complexity of implementation.

Table 4.2 outlines the phases of change and the mental barriers associated with engaging in these phases.

Running through the process of discovery, creating the case for change, and experimentation is to promote involvement. This may be in discussing the change with people considered "early adopters" or socializing and gathering feedback from individuals on drafts. The process of discovery can serve as a basis for successful involvement. If you've interviewed individuals in the organization, they can become "change champions" or part of a "guiding coalition." Promoting involvement seems obvious, but like discovery it can be overlooked given the opportunity costs. It's quicker to issue directives than promote involvement. Nevertheless, it is considered a standard best practice in leading planned change.

The three phases or best practices to leading change increase your probability of success but they can easily become overlooked in the name of efficiency. They are an investment in the success of your initiative. It takes time to engage in discovery, to be deliberate about creating the case for change, and to pursue an experimental strategy of small wins or losses.

Table 4.2 Phases of change and mental barriers to overcome

Phase of Change	Mental Barriers to Engaging in Phase
Engage in discovery	Certainty and overconfidence
Make a compelling case for change	Curse of knowledge
Take an experimental mindset	Overoptimism

Nevertheless, as we've seen in prior stories, not engaging in these activities can lead to failure.

Best practices for change can raise one's sense of efficacy, but there are constant political calculations and constraints that will be faced. Despite engaging in discovery, carefully making the case for change, and aiming for small wins or losses, you might still face resistance, as we saw with Maya and Kelly. In those cases, conviction is paramount. Believing in what you are trying to accomplish will help you face setbacks and resistance.

Summary

This chapter explored the process of leading change over time. We looked at best practices to consider when leading change, including:

1. Recognizing whether your change is voluntary or mandated (by senior executives) and using an appropriate set of tactics for either situation
2. Avoiding "psychological reactance" by promoting involvement
3. To prove your idea, sometimes taking a calculated risk to implement it without approval
4. Engaging in a process of discovery, which generates insights and develops empathy
5. Creating dissatisfaction with status quo by comprehensively describing the problem
6. Adopting an experimental mindset to learn from small wins or losses

Now that we've explored speaking up without formal authority, what if you are a team or organizational leader, how can you create a context that encourages employees to speak up about critical issues?

CHAPTER 5

Promoting Independent Thinking

This chapter explores ways to promote independent thinking in your team and organization. We'll explore a wide range of techniques and mindsets that can help you avoid groupthink and surface the best thinking within your team. This chapter differs from previous chapters in assuming you are in a position with formal authority within your group and/or organization.

Autocratic and Democratic Leadership Styles

As a leader, one of the biggest challenges in helping to promote independent thinking and speaking up is to overcome autocratic impulses. As Ray Dalio, the founder of one of the largest hedge funds in the world, writes in his book of management principles:

> Even the most benevolent leaders are prone to becoming more autocratic, if for no other reason than because managing a lot of people and having limited time to do it requires them to make numerous difficult choices quickly, and they sometimes lose patience with arguments and issue commands instead.[1]

Thus, there is an ever-present impulse to be more autocratic—an impulse that can be exacerbated by the situation, even if we are largely benevolent. But, if we want to encourage independent thinking and speaking up, we need to be more mindful of overcoming autocratic impulses and openly soliciting ideas from others. To openly solicit ideas from others is to be more democratic.

The distinction between autocratic and democratic leadership styles has a long history in applied psychology and was the focus of one of the founding fathers of the field, Kurt Lewin, who began studying leadership styles in the late 1930s.[2] Understanding the consequences of these styles was of great personal and practical importance to Lewin. He was born in Poland and lived in Germany throughout most of his life, serving in the German army in World War I. As a Jewish individual, he fortuitously left Germany in the early 1930s and worked the remainder of his career in the United States. As a scholar, he wanted to shed scientific light on the political turmoil that was happening in the world, such as the rise of Nazism in Germany. Thus, studying the effects of democratic and autocratic leadership was of utmost importance and an area of study that could use more precise evidence. As he asks in a 1939 publication, "Is not democratic group life more pleasant, but authoritarianism more efficient? These are the sorts of questions to which 'opinionated' answers are many and varied today, and to which scientific answers, are, on that account, all the more necessary."[3]

To study the effect of leadership styles, Lewin and colleagues experimentally created three "social climates"—authoritarian, democratic, and laissez-faire. To create these "social climates," an adult would act in accordance with one of the three styles while leading a group of 10-year-old boys. To be authoritarian, the leader would determine all the policies of the group and dictate the work task. To be democratic, the leader would encourage group discussion about policies and facilitate group decision making. Laissez-faire leadership allowed complete freedom for the group with little or no participation from the leader. Accordingly, a laissez-faire style of leadership was deemed so ineffective for group functioning that it was abandoned in future studies as a leadership style.[4] In Lewin's studies, they found that, with leaders present, performance was roughly equal between the autocratic and democratic groups, but when the leaders left, performance declined for those in the autocratic group but not in the democratic group.[5] They also found, as one might guess, more submission by group members to authoritarian leaders and a reliance on a leader for instructions and directions. Finally, they also observed more hostility in the autocratic compared to the democratic group, most notably when the leader was absent. Among many factors, Lewin and colleagues surmised this hostility between group members was a result of the "tension" created in the group (what we might now call "stress"). While Lewin and colleagues were interested in how leadership promoted hostility and aggression, a submissive and hostile environment doesn't foster individuals speaking their minds.

Although Lewin's studies were with children (with obvious drawbacks to interpreting the results in the workplace), the conceptual distinction between autocratic and democratic leaders was a major advance that helped leadership scholars in future decades. More recently, in a meta-analysis of 23 studies on the impact of autocratic and democratic leadership styles on productivity, democratic leadership was found to be more effective (compared to autocratic leadership) on "moderately or highly complex tasks."[6] In these tasks, you need to use the wisdom of the group in comparison to the dictates of a leader. In summarizing the field, John Gastil defined democratic leadership as "giving group members responsibility, improving the general abilities and leadership skills of other group members, and assisting the group in its decision-making process."[7] Table 5.1 is an outline of the key features of autocratic and democratic leadership in their "pure forms."

As outlined in Table 5.1, I offer a more charitable portrayal of autocratic leadership, of being directive and making decisions with little input from others, although it can be portrayed with stronger moral overtones. This includes being demeaning and abusive to subordinates and demanding loyalty and submissiveness.[8] This, of course, can be a dangerous form of autocratic leadership, but as noted, a central point of this chapter is about overcoming autocratic *impulses*, which even the most benevolent of us might have, given the circumstances. Thus, I am stressing how we might overcome being a "good-natured" autocrat who, for whatever reason, is slipping toward being too directive and making decisions with little or no deliberation from others.

While being autocratic or democratic is described in its pure form, we can, of course, switch styles given the dictates of the situation. When is being autocratic functional? When is being democratic functional? In a book about independent thinking, I'll argue that, on average, democratic

Table 5.1 Leadership Styles

	Autocratic (Directive)	Democratic (Participative)
Attributes/ outcomes	Makes decisions with little or no group deliberation	Facilitates group decision making
	Fosters submissiveness and disempowered employees	Empowers employees to take responsibility
	Less concern with fairness of decision-making process	Demonstrates a concern for procedural justice
	Rarely listens to employees	Shows a willingness to listen
Warranted in following conditions	Time pressure	Complex and difficult problems
	Leader has proven judgment/ expertise	Requisite knowledge is diffused throughout the group
	Lack of motivation among employees	
Hazards	Leader's judgment/expertise is faulty	Lengthened time for debate/ discussion
	Novel ideas/solutions are not surfaced	
	Submissiveness can lead to less self-directedness	
	Low sense of fairness and respect decreases employee satisfaction	

Source: Based on Lewin, Lippitt, and White (1939); Gastil (1994b).

leadership is more effective. However, in some instances, the situation may warrant autocratic impulses, especially if there is time pressure. In addition, a leader's judgment may be well grounded, given his or her experience in a domain, and thus their expertise and judgment are better than others. Although in some situations this may be true, in others you need to harness all the knowledge and expertise of a diverse group to make the best decision possible. This requires, of course, a realization that you don't know everything. A certain degree of intellectual humility is needed to realize that in some situations, but not all, the collective or majority will make a better decision than a single individual. This humility may be hard to come by but can often result from past failures where we realize our limitations.

This was true for Ray Dalio. In the early 1980s, Dalio was certain in his prediction that the United States was headed for a "depression." This would be substantially worse than a recession. As Dalio recalls:

> This view was extremely controversial. To most people, "depression" was a scary word used by kooky and sensationalist people, not something thoughtful people took seriously. But I had studied debt and depressions back to 1800, done my calculations, and was confident that the debt crisis led by emerging countries was coming.[9]

After Mexico defaulted on its debt in 1982, Dalio appeared before Congress to confidently deliver his prediction. He was also a guest on prominent television shows where he outlined his reasoning. In the end, however, he was "dead wrong." This taught him a powerful lesson. As he states, "My experience over this period was like a series of blows to the head with a baseball bat. Being so wrong—and especially so publicly wrong—was incredibly humbling and cost me just about everything I had built at Bridgewater."[10]

Going through such an experience makes you more wary of being highly confident in your predictions. In addition, as Dalio realized, you need to be open to challenges of where you are wrong. This realization moves you away from autocratic impulses and toward a more democratic form of leadership. To make fully informed decisions, you want to surface all the best thinking possible.

While we can be both autocratic and democratic given a situation, we are also likely to be predisposed to one style over another. In an overview of the factors increasing the likelihood of being autocratic, Peter Harms of the University of Alabama and his colleagues outline several factors. These include, among others, being less agreeable, having a high need for power, being less emotionally stable (e.g., suspicious), and being narcissistic.[11] These are suggestive traits that impact one's likelihood of being autocratic, but, to my knowledge, there is no definitive account of the life experiences that predispose someone to be autocratic. It would be a complex mix of someone's inherited predispositions, life history, and situational conditions that would create autocratic behavior in its extreme forms (although, as mentioned, I think it's most important to be aware of autocratic impulses in their moderate, everyday forms).

There is another reason to be more of a democratic leader: it increases team member satisfaction. This is for a variety of reasons including that, on average, people like to have their voices heard. However, even if we voice our point of view, we don't always prevail; nevertheless, we at least want a "fair audience." This is commonly called procedural justice. Procedural justice is our sense of fairness about the process that was used to make a decision. It includes whether you think you had a chance to share your perspective, defend your point of view, whether you were listened to, and so on. Procedural justice is analogous to whether there is "due process," which is a legal and constitutional term, but we have similar judgments about the process of decision making in organizations. As one interviewee commented:

> Now if you're my boss and I have a responsibility to tell you how I feel, you respect that and you can say, "Look, Tom, great, but we're going to go this way." …my responsibility as a boss is to give everybody on my team a fair audience. Please disagree with me, but if I make the decision we're going to go that way, then you've got to support it. As long as I'm giving you a fair audience, that's fair.

There are several ideas in this statement. First is having a felt sense of responsibility to state how you feel about an issue and, when done, there is respect given for stating your opinion. As studies have found there is "value-expressive" worth of being able to voice one's perspective, even if an expressed point of view does not influence a final decision.[12] Providing a "fair audience" is also a sign of respect, and if you feel respected as a member of an organization, you are more likely to support decisions and work toward them, even if you don't initially agree.[13]

In a comprehensive review of studies that examined outcome favorability and procedural justice, the researchers found that even if outcome favorability was low (i.e., you lost the decision), if there was a sense of fairness in the process, the favorability of one's reaction is *almost* as high as if you "won" the decision.[14] For example, imagine Tim and Sue are vying for resources for their department for a new hire. You could make the decision autocratically and just tell Sue she'll be getting the resources and Tim finds out he lost. In this scenario, Tim is both upset by the outcome and upset about an unfair process. If, instead, you have a process for both Tim and Sue to outline their proposed course of action and why they need a new hire, even if Tim doesn't win the additional resources, he'll view the decision *almost* as favorably as Sue. Tim, of course, has to view the process as fair, and not biased from the start as a sham.

The researchers who compiled this result from over 45 studies hypothesized that part of the barrier to creating a fair process is that it increases the psychological burden on decision makers. As they summarize,

> procedural justice is likely to reduce the psychological distance between the implementers and the recipients of a resource allocation decision. Implementers, however, may wish to maintain distance. By keeping their distance, they may minimize feelings of guilt associated with doing bad things to good people.[15]

In this case, you don't want to give Tim and Sue a fair hearing, because you'd rather not agonize over the decision, and you don't want the burden of feeling guilty for your actions. Better to keep your distance, make the decision autocratically and move on.

Again, this is the seductive allure of autocratic leadership. But you are giving up the opportunity of making a better decision by allowing everyone a chance to speak up, and you are decreasing the satisfaction with the decision by members of your team who are losing out. Thus, being more democratic is to be more aware of giving everyone a "fair audience." You do so not only because it leads to instrumental gains to improve the decision but also because of the "value-expressive" worth of letting people share their point of view.

You might argue that a democratic leadership style will foster a climate of continual dissent and disagreement. In fact, it might create a fractious, conflict-abundant organization with little sense of cohesiveness. This brings to mind Aristotle's golden mean, where you try to avoid the excesses of either extreme. I have largely offered a narrative to avoid the extreme of excessive conformity, in particular given our tendency to accept authority. However, a fractious culture with employees empowered to speak their mind is certainly possible.[16] This risks a culture with little sense of alignment where there is constant disagreement and dissenting opinions, however tangential they might be.

To work together effectively, we need some shared understanding and a sense of alignment. "Alignment" is a common buzzword, and it's generally a good thing, meaning we need to be rowing in the same direction, with some common behaviors in the pursuit of a strategic goal. However, it's a fine line between advocacy of alignment and demanding conformity. One way to think about integrating alignment and independent thinking is to build alignment on top of a foundation of independent thinking. You want alignment to be the result of hashing things out, getting in sync about issues, and having the best ideas voiced. A democratic leadership style can help you build alignment *from* independent thinking—allowing individuals to state their viewpoints and then charting a path forward. This is in contrast to alignment based on conformity, where individuals are too afraid to dissent and dutifully comply. Autocratic behaviors are likely to lead to compliance and conformity. This is efficient in the short term, but it doesn't win the "hearts and minds" of employees.

Building alignment *from* independent thinking (rather than conformity) is a common challenge of any team leader, as Satya Nadella, who began as the CEO of Microsoft in 2014, states:

> Articulating our core raison d'etre and business was a good first step. But I also needed to get the right people on the bus to join me in leading these changes…The senior leadership team needed to become a cohesive team that shared a common worldview…I don't mean yes-men and yes-women. Debate and argument are essential. Improving upon each other's ideas is crucial. I wanted people to speak up. "Oh, here's a customer segmentation study I've done." "Here's a pricing approach that contradicts this idea." It's great to have a good, old-fashioned college debate. But there also has to be high quality agreement.[17]

Here we see an explicit desire to avoid "yes-men" and "yes-women" and an explicit statement that he wants people to "speak up." In addition, he wants "high quality agreement." It is a balancing act, with a demo-cratic approach aiming for more debate, but with the intent of that debate being alignment on a way forward. This contrasts with a leadership style that autocratically aims for alignment based on conformity.

Figure 5.1 contrasts these two forms of alignment: alignment based on conformity and alignment based on independent thinking.

This may sound naïve, however, as alignment may not magically emerge out of encouraging employee voice. There will be differing opin-ions and sometimes no consensus will emerge. Situations will often be resolved by the exercise of judgment, based on the person in a position of authority. Cynically, situations are simply resolved by the exercise of power, and, you might argue, this will ultimately lead to disillusionment—if employees are asked to speak up, but their perspectives are not acted upon. Again, this discounts the worth of having a "fair audience" and the value of having your voice heard even if you are not immediately persua-sive. As mentioned previously, research has found that individuals, even if they get an unfavorable outcome, are largely satisfied if they believe the process was fair.

While those in a position of authority bear the responsibility to create a climate of speaking up, employees need to help avoid the extreme of constant dissent and disagreement—for central to speaking up is know-ing when not to speak up. We can't be constantly sharing what is on our mind. As one individual discussed, you have to be able to distin-guish between a "thought and a well-formulated point-of-view." Another individual mentioned that he'd stay silent "even though I felt that the decisions were wrong in certain cases, I knew where it wasn't going to do any good for me to speak up. I'd already had a chance to say my piece, if

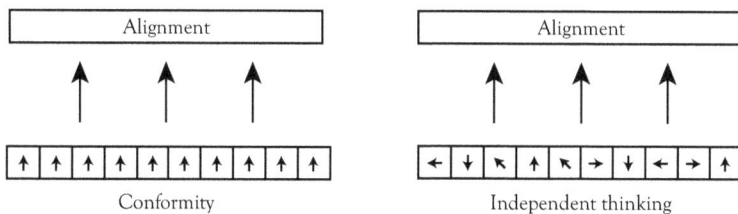

Figure 5.1 Alignment based on conformity versus alignment based on independent thinking

you will." There is an ever-present balance of "picking your battles" and sharing your view of reality but being willing to implement a course of action even if your point of view doesn't prevail.

One of the clearest distinctions to help avoid extremes of silent conformity over constant dissent is to be clear about periods of deliberation in comparison to periods of implementation and execution. During periods of deliberation, divergent views and speaking up are actively encouraged, but debate cannot continue endlessly. In periods of implementation, it's better to give ideas a chance. Of course, this assumes that work can be neatly split into deliberation and implementation. In much of what we do, we may always be in both, and during implementation we still need to speak up with critical information. However, in some situations, there may be a relatively clear distinction between a deliberation period and postdecision phase where speaking up constantly will be counterproductive.

In addition to whether, as a leader, you have a more autocratic or democratic leadership style is the expectation and acceptance of such a leadership style. Our implicit attitude in this regard is known as one's "power distance orientation." As individuals, largely based on our upbringing and societal norms, we have a power distance orientation, which is "the extent to which the less powerful members of organizations accept and expect that power is distributed unequally."[18] In studies of national culture, this has been measured by whether employees are afraid to express disagreement with their manager and whether there is an expectation of being consulted about decisions.[19] Questions to measure power distance include: "in most situations, managers should make decisions without consulting their subordinates"; "in work-related matters, managers have a right to expect obedience from their subordinates"; and "employees should not express disagreements with their managers."[20]

By and large, our power distance orientation is an implicit attitude—we show deference to authority or expect an egalitarian relationship—without awareness. Our orientation becomes salient when interacting with individuals from different national cultures that have, on average, a different power distance orientation. Countries where employees score high on power distance (i.e., are more accepting of power differences) include Malaysia and Russia, along with most Asian and Eastern

European countries. Low power distance countries include Austria, Israel, and Denmark, with the United States among the bottom quartile of low power distance countries (i.e., expecting an egalitarian relationship).[21] What is important to consider is the variation in cultural acceptance of more autocratic or democratic leadership styles based on the power distance orientation of a society.

In sum, we all have autocratic impulses. We need to become aware of such impulses and retain humility to facilitate a democratic process of decision making when it is warranted.

Tactics to Promote Independent Thinking and Avoid Groupthink

In being less autocratic and directive, you can also avoid groupthink. Groupthink is a well-known term and often invoked when it seems like there is easy agreement on a complex decision. The term was popularized by Irving Janis with the 1972 publication of *Victims of Groupthink: A Psychological Study of Foreign-Policy Decisions and Fiascos.* In the book, Janis uses several high-profile government decisions that went awry, the most prominent of which was John F. Kennedy's Bay of Pigs invasion of Cuba in 1961. To briefly summarize, the United States backed an invasion of Cuba by 1,400 Cuban exiles. The exiles had landed in Cuba near the Bay of Pigs to help overthrow Fidel Castro who had come to power two years earlier. Castro was supported by the Soviet Union and he was building a communist country—a movement the United States was seeking to contain during the Cold War. When the 1,400 exiles landed near the Bay of Pigs, Castro was ready for them and the exiles quickly surrendered after a day of fighting. Over 100 exiles were killed and 1,100 captured.[22]

Irving Janis wondered how a group of highly intelligent individuals could have collectively advised JFK to make such a decision. His answer was "groupthink." Groupthink happens when "members' strivings for unanimity override their motivation to realistically appraise alternative courses of action."[23] Janis chose the word "groupthink" to be consonant with Orwellian terms such as "doublethink."[24] To Janis, this was to give groupthink an "invidious connotation." As he says, "The invidiousness is intentional: Groupthink refers to a deterioration of mental efficiency, reality testing, and moral judgment that results from in-group pressures."[25]

In social psychology, a cousin term to groupthink is *pluralistic ignorance*—an analogous experience to groupthink where individuals insufficiently surface their preferences. Studies of pluralistic ignorance focus on individuals withholding their private views because of an erroneous belief that there is unanimous agreement. While that may be true for groupthink, studies of pluralistic ignorance predate Janis' coining of the term groupthink, and, for groupthink, a directive leader is central to the account of faulty decision making (which is not the case for pluralistic ignorance).[26]

A story often used to illustrate pluralistic ignorance is the Abilene Paradox.[27] The story is of a family at home on a hot day in Texas. One member of the family proposes driving in a car with no air conditioning to have dinner in Abilene, Texas. Everyone mistakenly thinks everyone else prefers this course of action, and the family ends up taking the trip. To the dismay of everyone involved when they return, no one really wanted to go. As the narrator summarizes:

> Here we were, four reasonably sensible people who, of our own volition, had just taken a 106-mile trip across a godforsaken desert in a furnace-like temperature through a cloud-like dust storm to eat unpalatable food at a hole-in-the-wall cafeteria in Abilene, when none of us had really wanted to go.[28]

The anecdote is amusing given its resonance of "going along" even though our private preference contradicts our public behavior. When enough individuals falsely believe that everyone's public actions reveal their private preferences, the group continues in a direction that no one prefers. In a more recent study, James Westphal and Michael Bednar found among a sample of 228 corporate boards of mid-sized companies that "individual directors overattribute a lack of expressed concern among their colleagues to confidence in the current strategy."[29] Similar to the family erroneously taking a trip to Abilene, they found that in many cases, especially among low-performing firms, directors assumed that if others were *not* expressing a concern, then everyone was confident in the course of action.

So how can you overcome groupthink and pluralistic ignorance to promote independent thinking in your team or organization? In addition to overcoming autocratic impulses, the following section outlines key tactics to promote independent thinking and avoid groupthink.

Avoid Stating Your Position First and Remain Open-Minded

One of the key risks of groupthink is having a directed leader with known preferences.[30] In these circumstances, individuals will often conform to the leader's point of view. As a leader, as best as you can, don't start a meeting by stating your position. Let others speak first before stating your position. Even better, signal open-mindedness.

For example, in making billion-dollar investments, Ray Dalio states being "radically open-minded" is one of his key management principles. As he states: "Radical open-mindedness is the ability to effectively explore different points of view and different possibilities…It requires you to replace your attachment to always being right with the joy of learning what's true."[31]

Open-mindedness has also been researched by many psychologists. In a comprehensive review of how to assess "good thinking" in the book *The Rationality Quotient* (by Keith Stanovich, Richard West, and Maggie Toplak), what emerges again and again is actively open-minded thinking. Stanovich and colleagues measure actively open-minded thinking with several items, including: "Beliefs should always be revised in response to new information or evidence" and "I like to gather many different types of evidence before I decide what to do."[32]

Open-mindedness is a cognitive aspiration that is at odds with a cluster of thinking habits, including our desire to be "right," a need for cognitive efficiency (i.e., not constantly rethinking every position), and a desire to defend against threats to our self-competence. There are limits to being open-minded, of course, and we need not listen and engage in every opposing viewpoint. As Stanovich and colleagues describe, being actively open-minded is not a disposition to maximize. However, we tend to be deficient in open-mindedness such that more is better.

A concern for being open-minded is often demonstrated through a willingness to listen. As one former CEO of a Fortune 500 company describes:

> I also spent a lot of informal time with the organization. I'd go and do business reviews and stuff, and then we'd always go out to dinner, and I would talk to people. And for whatever reason, I don't know why, I always have been amazed at what people would tell me in an informal session that....I would think, "Gosh, I don't think I would ever share that if I was this person, to the CEO of the company." So you have to kind of respect that, right? You have to listen. You have to be open to hearing things. Sometimes you don't wanna hear them. Sometimes they're stupid, the ideas, but you have to show a willingness to listen to the organization and even sometimes be willing to let them try things, as long as they're not gonna kill the enterprise, to see if things will work or not. That's just sort of a judgment, you know?

Here, we see a former CEO being candid that his first instinct was to judge ideas as "stupid." Rather than be dismissive, he let employees discuss their ideas and maybe even implement some of them as long as they wouldn't "kill the enterprise." In being open-minded, he might be *wrong,* and the ideas will be successful, as no one is omniscient. At the very least, however, this approach creates an environment where people feel heard and can speak up with different ideas.

Similarly, I interviewed an officer in the military who said that if his first instinct was to disagree with an idea, rather than say, "I don't agree," he would ask, "What line of logic...what is making us come to this conclusion? Why are you approaching it in this manner? What assumptions are we making? What kind of information are we using to lead us down this path?" In this way, he would give individuals a chance to describe their approach to avoid defensiveness from blunt disagreement. He did this to make individuals more "comfortable" with having conversations, rather than being direct, blunt, and autocratic. Here, we see a practical way to exhibit humility as a leader: If your first impulse is to disagree and begin issuing directives, instead ask questions to explore the logic. Perhaps you are misinformed or only have a partial understanding of the issue and may be persuaded. It also signals to your direct reports a greater degree of psychological safety in exploring issues with you.

Thus, the first tactic to avoiding groupthink is also one of the most obvious but nevertheless crucial. Be less directive, avoid stating your position first, and aim for open-mindedness through listening and asking questions.

Communicate the Expectation for Independent Thinking

In addition to being open-minded, you can encourage independent thinking by making it an expectation. In an interview with an individual who works at an investment firm, he said, on his first day, the founder of the firm gives everyone a five-minute talk. The founder outlines four fundamental principles of work: the first being investment performance, the second being to "go out of your way to satisfy the client," the third to "always act with integrity in everything you do. Stay away from gray areas," and the fourth was that

> at any time, if you ever see anything that doesn't make sense to you, or think, "Geez, there's a better way to do that," or "This is stupid. Why do we do things this way?" Just walk right into the person's office…and just say, ask them if they ever thought of doing it a different way. Do it diplomatically, but you know, just go in and suggest a better way.

The founder continued by saying, "If you don't do that, then you're not doing your job."

Given this talk on his first day, Brian, a member of the firm for many years, states that, "So that last thing has really, kind of set the tone, I guess. From day one, I felt very comfortable, very comfortable being a… declining voice, being comfortable just allows you a different—an out-of-consensus viewpoint on something." Brian says,

> Sometimes when I do have a differing viewpoint on a small thing, I'll always preface, before I say that I disagree with you on this, or have you thought about this, I always say, "On my first day, you told me if I ever had a differing viewpoint to walk right in and say it."

This expectation paid dividends years later when the firm was considering taking over the business of a nearby mutual fund. The founder considered it an excellent idea, as if it was free business from his friends and nearby acquaintances. As Brian states, "it had a meaningful amount of revenue tied to it." Brian, however, viewed it as a risky proposition, including potential damage to the firm's reputation and performance. The mutual fund had many prior years of poor performance and this record would be linked with their firm.

Brian, along with several others, eventually prevailed in outlining the reasons against taking over the mutual fund. As he states, "Eventually, after we talked about it…there was more doubts that came out, then…it became clear that it was not going to happen. It just kind of died under its own weight." In this, we can see the value of empowering individuals and setting an expectation for independent thinking. This was created through direct one-on-one interactions during the first week of being on the job. Messages sent at this time can be highly salient for individuals, as we see with Brian, and it empowered him to dissent. While we do not know the counterfactual of the firm acquiring the mutual fund, by all accounts, the expectations that were set on day one paid dividends in creating a culture where dissent was encouraged.

Promote Accountability to "Get at the Truth"

Another way to increase independent thinking is to promote the social norm to "get at the truth" and have individuals explain and justify their reasoning. In one study that tested this hypothesis, the researchers had individuals primed for either "getting along" or "getting at the truth" by reading different scenarios.[33] The researchers primed individuals by having them read a scenario that described either a search for truth or when your behavior needed to be tailored to the situation.[34] For example, in the "getting at the truth" scenario, you would read about a reporter trying to get the facts of a story. For "getting along," participants read a scenario about being on a blind date set up by a close friend, but quickly realizing there was little attraction. After reading each of the scenarios, participants were asked what actions they would take in that scenario. For example, if they read the scenario about being a reporter, an individual might suggest going to the library to look up facts or speaking with an expert.

After reading the scenarios, participants had to allocate a marketing budget between an American and European lager. If participants had been primed with the "getting at the truth" scenario, they were more likely to choose the option that provided an "objectively better return on marketing investment." However, if they were primed with the "getting along" scenario, they were more influenced by the choice of their discussion partner, regardless of whether it led to an objectively better return on marketing investment. The positive effect of being primed to "get at the truth" was most pronounced when participants had to "explain and justify" their decision (i.e., being held accountable). Accountability has many connotations but it can mean having to explain your reasoning for a decision, perhaps in a meeting.[35]

As the researchers conclude:

> Accountability to an audience whose preferences are known does not invariably doom people to subpar decisions that are biased by conformity pressures. If people are focused on the goal of making accurate decisions when they are accountable, the quality of their decision-making increases as compared to when people are not accountable or to when people have the goal of getting along.[36]

These results are a hopeful antidote to the conformity pressures discussed throughout this book (and found in most social psychology experiments). So how do you foster a motivation to "get at the truth" in an organization? At Bridgewater Associates, one of the world's largest hedge funds, there is a constant refrain and insistence that employees think for themselves and ask "Is it true?"[37] Likewise, when I spoke with a Chief Investment Officer at a different hedge fund, he set up a monthly meeting with his direct report who would have to answer the question, "What is something you don't think I want to hear, but you think is true?" Over time, this helped promote the notion of "getting at the truth" over "getting along," and there was accountability because the CIO's direct report knew that at each monthly meeting, he'd be asked the question.

Thus, while "truth" is a battered term (especially in postmodern philosophy), as a practical matter, we have a sense of whether we are being candid and moving beyond superficial explanations.[38] The use of the term "truth" implies being candid, expressing doubts, and critically evaluating claims. In setting it as a norm, we can improve decision making and avoid conformity.

Critically Evaluating Ideas on Their Merits (Not Their Source)

Another consideration to promote independent thinking is to evaluate arguments based on their merits, rather than accepting arguments based on status or authority. This was the case for Alan who had strong arguments for his position but was arguing against a high-status member. At the time of being interviewed, Alan's consulting firm was in the process of dismantling its "practice areas," a structure the firm had converted to close to a decade earlier. Practice areas were meant to promote thought leadership about an industry, such as education or global health. The idea to reorganize into practice areas was proposed many years earlier by a board member of Alan's consulting firm. This board member was a partner of a much bigger consulting firm which had 50 or 60 offices around the globe and hundreds of partners. In contrast, Alan's firm had around 15 partners in two locations, and his firm didn't aspire to become such a large firm, as they serve a niche market.

When it was argued to reorganize into "practice areas," Alan argued that it didn't make sense for a firm their size to go in that direction. Alan argued that they should be organized around capabilities, such as strategy and financial sustainability, not practice areas that would be too focused on industry knowledge. As Alan states, "People come to us not because we're experts in the issues. Our clients are the experts in the issues. They come to us, because we understand strategy, and or development…All those sort of cross cutting capabilities." Alan's viewpoint wasn't persuasive enough in comparison to the board member. As he recalls, "it was like me versus her, and they're like, who are you?"

From that point forward, the firm spent an enormous amount of time and effort developing "practice areas." This included meetings two or three times a year along with yearly plans that seemed to have little impact. Alan also saw that any practice area would be highly contingent upon the clients they happened to be working with. For example, they had a large education foundation as a client, and thus formed an "education practice," but once that education foundation was no longer working with Alan's firm, it's "like we've had a ghost town of a practice for the past five years."

Alan was also frustrated because the focus on practice areas meant they weren't investing time in building their intellectual property in their cross-cutting capabilities such as strategy. Instead, they were investing their time on issues specific to an industry, and "We shouldn't be the ones trying to point out what's the most effective curriculum for a charter school. And that's the direction we were headed by organizing our own practice area." While these practice areas were in place for close to a decade, the tipping point for their eventual dismantling was losing project work, especially when the firm was in direct competition with another firm for a project. "We were starting to lose because our capabilities were stale. And they started to realize like, holy crap, this is because we haven't been investing in our capabilities. We've been investing in these issues, like being smart on education."

For Alan, this experience, along with several others, made him feel like the experience of independent thinking "is just like shouting into the wind." He continues, "I don't get that excited about expressing independent thoughts these days, because it just feels like it's not going to go very far." As in Alan's case, those in positions of authority can impose a new direction for an organization that hasn't emerged from reasoned debate. This isn't news, but if you want to have a prosperous organization, you want to make the best decisions possible. Think of the years and thousands of dollars Alan's firm spent organizing into practice areas, only to discard the idea many years later. Alan can at least take solace that he didn't think it was a good idea and he spoke up about it. Alternatively, he could have remained silent. Then, he'd be both dismayed by the outcome and regret his inaction.

Alan's story mirrors many others where a course of action is chosen with questionable wisdom and then continues based on inertia and status quo pressures. During deliberating a course of action, it highlights how you want to decouple the merit of an idea from its source. In this case, the idea of practice areas was more readily accepted because it was being made by a board member. It also appears that the idea of practice areas lasted too long and was not dismantled until the situation hit a crisis point. While we should give ideas a fair chance to be implemented and not be questioned all along the way, it is likely many people had similar doubts about the structure far sooner. However, there were vested interests in keeping the status quo as people were hired to run the practice areas. These are lessons for those in a position with formal authority. It is not letting ideas be unduly implemented merely because a high-status member advocates for them. It is being proactively agile to question whether a current initiative "makes sense." And it is making sure the merits of ideas are heard before there is widespread disengagement.

Structured Ideation Process

Another way to be more democratic and promote speaking up is to use a structured ideation process such as the nominal group technique or "brainwriting."[39] The process, at its simplest, involves everyone writing their ideas on a Post-it Note in silence prior to group discussion. After this short period of individual writing (around five minutes), each person suggests one idea in a round-robin fashion. Discussion and evaluation of ideas are meant to occur after all the ideas are posted or written on a whiteboard. This process easily translates to virtual meetings where ideas can be typed in a chat box after individuals generate ideas. Although it might seem odd or uncomfortable to sit in silence as a group for five minutes, the benefits are a wide array of ideas being shared.

This process avoids the common pitfall of the group anchoring on the first suggestion made, and as previously discussed, if the first suggestion is the leader's idea, conformity is likely to follow. Given the expectation to generate *many* ideas, the process helps overcome group conformity. There is a more diverse set of ideas to evaluate and discuss. Brainwriting also helps to equalize discussion among introverts and extraverts by mitigating the excesses of individuals who tend to dominate the discussion at the expense of quieter voices.

Company (or Devil's) Advocate

Another means to break conformity is to structure dissent within a role. This includes the well-known use of a "devil's advocate."[40] The term was coined by the Catholic church in the 1500s to structure dissent into the process of granting sainthood. Understandably, few individuals would want to make arguments against someone for sainthood. Yet, without some counterarguments, most individuals would be approved. Similarly, most of us want to get along and support something that is relatively good. There is little personal benefit of offering counterarguments in these cases, and often negative outcomes to the individual, such as being disdained or perceived as disagreeable. In addition, the negative outcomes of poor decisions are uncertain and diffused over time (e.g., granting sainthood to too many individuals). With accountability diffused, there is little incentive for the reputational risk of dissenting. Structuring dissent into a role, however, can counter these disincentives. It increases viewpoint diversity while also mitigating against reputational damage.

Kevin Schnieders, the CEO of the workforce development company Educational Data System Inc. (EDSI), says they prefer to have someone play the role of "company advocate." As he states:

> I kept hearing people say, when they had a different opinion, they would say, "Well, I'm going to play devil's advocate." And after I reflected about that, I'm like, who wants to take on the role of the devil? …I started asking them to call it the EDSI advocate… What you're really doing is hearing an idea that you don't think is good for the company, and you're advocating on behalf of the company. So, it's absolutely okay to have a different idea. We want that. Why don't we just call it the EDSI advocate?

In their case, the company's culture, by and large, was very positive and agreeable, but, as Kevin Schnieders states, one individual "just sees it differently, right? He sees the glass half empty, if you will." But the process of dissenting became easier with renaming the role. "He'll raise his hand

and say, 'Hey, I'm just going to be the EDSI advocate for a minute here. Do we really think that's the best course of action? Do we think that's the best tactic to take?'" As Kevin continues,

> so I think that little subtle change of just renaming something has helped people really gravitate towards the idea that...yeah, I can have a different opinion here. It doesn't have to fall in line with the group, because I'm advocating in the right way on behalf of the company.

Direct Solicitation

Another means of avoiding groupthink is also perhaps the most obvious: direct solicitation. This may be prior to a meeting, during, or after, but it is being aware that individuals may be self-censoring and then drawing out their opinions. Kevin Schnieders at EDSI utilizes this approach. He states,

> I'm fascinated by the quieter people and making sure that their voice is heard. So independently as a leader, I'm trying to seek those people out before the meeting. And say, ask, just ask them.... Do you want to talk for a couple minutes before we go in there, maybe more comfortable one-on-one then in front of 10 people?

This tactic requires a willingness and desire to hear from quieter individuals. It is done with a recognition that—at least in the deliberation phase—the more viewpoint diversity the better to improve decision making.

Structuring Debates Rather Than Disagreement

A final way to help promote information sharing is to frame a conversation as a debate rather than a disagreement. For example, researchers tested participants' response to receiving two different messages: "I see we have different opinions about the best acquisition target. I expect that we'll have a debate [disagreement] about the pros and cons of acquiring the different companies."[41] They found that use of the term debate created a perception that the individual was open to dissenting opinions and thus individuals were more open to sharing information about their perspective. Likewise, imagine in a meeting when someone says, "I disagree." It is usually in a forceful tone and doesn't lead to a thoughtful back-and-forth, but signals that someone has firmly made up their mind.

As a leader, you might say, "Does anyone *disagree* with our course of action?" Or, "Let's *debate* the course of action." The second framing suggests an openness and receptivity to hear different viewpoints. It also encourages people to share their viewpoints for the "sake of argument." You can also structure debates by having teams prepare contrasting positions in advance, as we saw in Chapter 1 with two teams taking opposing positions on overhauling their performance management system. While language is suggestive, and reframing a deep-seated disagreement as a "debate" won't be a panacea, the framing connotes an open conversation and desire to articulate all the facets of a decision.

Summary

In sum, this chapter outlined several specific ways to promote independent thinking to avoid groupthink. They include:

1. Overcoming autocratic impulses to be intentionally democratic
2. Avoiding stating your position first
3. Remaining open-minded, often signaled through a willingness to listen
4. Setting the expectation for independent thinking
5. Promoting the social norm to "get at the truth"
6. Aiming to critically evaluate ideas on their merits (not their source)
7. Using a structured ideation process such as brainwriting
8. Using a "company" or devil's advocate
9. Directly soliciting ideas, especially from quieter individuals
10. Framing conflict as a debate rather than disagreement

All of these tactics help build alignment on a foundation of independent thinking, rather than on a foundation of compliance and conformity. Of course, you have to authentically care about listening to and learning from others. These "tactics" signal an underlying predisposition of humility and respect for others, thereby helping you avoid groupthink to make better decisions.

CHAPTER 6

Regretting Inaction and the Road Ahead

This final chapter explores the role of regret and whether, over the long term, we regret taking action more than doing nothing. In addition to exploring what the psychology of regret teaches us, we'll look at self-efficacy, including its sources, as we explore the road ahead. Let's first look at a story of regretting inaction.

Regretting Inaction

Sharon was head of a $30 million account for a global marketing firm and was leading a global campaign for a well-known consumer product. The client voiced repeated concern that the project team Sharon was leading did not have sufficient global expertise. Sharon agreed but faced a dilemma. While the firm had offices throughout the world, the account was structured so that nearly all the $30 million accrued to the New York office.[1] To get adequate global expertise on the project, she would have to restructure the revenue so that larger portions of the revenue would go to international offices to pay for their creative support and time. Sharon wrote a proposal for restructuring the project and spoke with several international offices about how it might work. She had worked under a global contract before and knew how to structure such an account.

Sharon met with her direct boss to review the plan. As she recounts,

> I kind of took her through the thoughts, and made it seem in much more draft form than it really was. It was actually fairly well baked, at least in my own mind, but I wanted to get her to feel like

she could help create this with me. She didn't really provide a lot of input frankly, but we got this thing to a place where it could be presented to management, the powers that be.

Sharon knew that it would be "bad news" to the New York office that they would "lose a bit of revenue," but the cost of inaction, in her mind, was potentially losing the account, given the repeated interactions she had with the client who was asking for greater global expertise.

After a second conversation with her boss, Sharon asked, "What are our next steps? Who do we want to take this too?" Her boss replied, "Well, just leave it with me and I'll run it up the food chain." A couple of weeks passed and Sharon did not hear of any potential change. She followed up with her boss to ask about the proposal. As Sharon recalls,

> she basically said to just let it lie, to not do anything with it. And so I said, "Okay. Would you want to tell me why?" And she said, "It's going to create too much political firestorm for us. Let's just pretend like we never had this idea. Pretend like you never had this idea, we never came up with any of this."

Sharon never heard anything else about the document and basically "folded on the whole thing." She speculates that the proposal was used against her for wanting "to take revenue out of New York." However, as Sharon states, "[this] was just part of the story. What I really wanted to do was run the business correctly, not take money out of New York." A few months later Sharon decided to leave the organization based on a "toxic workplace" and repeated negative interactions with her boss—a boss who was fired several months after Sharon left. Upon reflection, Sharon says:

> I often think about what if we had done the right thing, and instead of stopping with her what if I had…I don't know. I had better relationships with some of the people, the senior most people [at headquarters] and tried to talk to them about it… [my boss] might have felt I was going behind her back, but at the end of the day I left and she's out of there anyway, and the right

thing didn't happen. The account, as far as I know, still isn't structured in a way that would make sense.

When asked what she learned from the incident, Sharon responds:

I just stuck with my boss and tried to sell it into her. I think I probably could have gone around her to more senior people and that would have ultimately probably been good for me because they would have seen I had a lot of operational skillsets that they probably weren't seeing because I just didn't get a lot of exposure to them…So, it was kind of a missed opportunity for me not to…at least try to have those conversations…I feel like if I had been a little more straightforward with knowing the New York office is a factor, and the management is a factor there I might as well have tried to have had one-on-one meetings with the New York president about it, about what I was thinking.

Here, we see Sharon regretting being overly deferential to her boss. It is an understandable impulse and one we are advised to follow, but while it may be reasonable advice in a majority of cases, in some circumstances it will prove unproductive.[2] As in Sharon's case, she regrets not being more transparent and open about her proposal and more freely discussing it with those in senior management positions. It's hard to know whether things would have worked out differently if Sharon had been openly transparent about her proposal. Perhaps the loss of revenue for those in power in the New York office would have been too threatening. Or, they'd agree that the risk of losing the $30 million account was too high and they needed to restructure the account like Sharon was recommending. Or, the message and proposal could have been conveyed to those who had the global interests of the firm in mind and they would have seen the reasonableness of the proposal and how it would facilitate better results for the client. We don't know. What we do know is that Sharon regrets not giving it a chance.

But what is regret, exactly? Regret is the "negative, cognitively based emotion that we experience when realizing or imagining that our present situation would have been better had we acted differently."[3] It involves a counterfactual realization of missed opportunities or embarrassment over an action we've taken. To examine regret, psychologists have distinguished between two forms, differentiated by their temporal distance from the situation. One is "hot regret" and the other "wistful regret."[4] Hot regret is the negative emotion we experience from a situation (usually something we've done that deviates from social norms) and it usually subsides over time.[5] Wistful regret, in contrast, is the realization of lost opportunities, and usually these lost opportunities can't be rectified. We can see wistful regret in Sharon's case, as she describes what she might have done differently.

Over the long term, with wistful regret, we often regret *inaction* more than action, especially as the consequences of inaction become more recognizable over time.[6] The psychologists Thomas Gilovich and Victoria Medvic outline several reasons why time increases the salience of regrettable *inaction*. First, with the benefit of time, the fears and doubts that plagued us in the moment are less prominent. Their hold over us becomes more inexplicable when we are far removed from the incident and have more retrospective confidence. This leads to the question, "why didn't I at least try?"[7] As Harvard psychologist Daniel Gilbert describes, we have "a more difficult time manufacturing positive and credible views of inactions than of actions."[8] It can be hard to justify inaction, partly because we become different people as we age, having successfully faced many challenges. Our "present self" can be more confident than our "past self." Thus, past *inactions* are hard to explain given who we are in the present.

Second, the consequences of action are relatively finite. They are bounded by what *actually happened*. In contrast, what *might have happened* is essentially infinite. "They are bounded only by one's imagination."[9] This means we can readily imagine counterfactuals had we taken some action. We might have been promoted, for example, or had a variety of successful outcomes. This leads to a conclusion bounded by the specifics of any situation: We are, on average, better off taking more action than less. In Sharon's case, this definitely seems true. She would have gotten exposure to senior leadership and if it wasn't possible to restructure the account, she would have received a definitive answer and learned why it wouldn't work.

While Sharon's example teaches us how we regret inaction, *antici-pating* regret can also lead us to make the difficult decision of speaking up. Let's look at the story of a whistleblower who was motivated by the anticipation of regret.

In the late 1990s, Wendy Addison was the treasurer of a South African company called LeisureNet (a fitness club company).[10] She had been at the company for over eight years and was the only woman on the senior executive team. Over time, she noticed a gradual increase of "lawful but awful" behaviors and a "hubristic, maverick" attitude. One day, she became troubled by the request from the joint CEOs of the company that she should transfer hundreds of millions of South African rand to New Jersey (when the legal limit was 50,000 rand). To transfer this sum of money overseas would have been a "breach of legal caveat" and the company had no business in New Jersey. The legal limit was put into place to help South Africa by keeping money within the economy. This request to transfer money wasn't ambiguous or something that could be rationalized. As Wendy says, "This amount of money was outside of that legal caveat, no matter what I was being told, I knew that it was outside this legal caveat. I then also knew that we were breaking the law."

Why was she being asked to do this? In questioning the request, she was met with "purposeful obfuscation" and she had to decide what to do. As she says:

> I got to the point where having met with all this purposeful obfus-cation, I considered my long-term future and I didn't expect what that would be, but I also thought about myself as a good moral person and I considered what I might be telling my son, who was 12 at the time, five years hence what part in the story as it unfolds would I choose to take and that was one of the salient points for me to pick up the phone and make an anonymous phone call to the South African Exchange Control Board.[11]

Wendy, who is unusually introspective, says anticipating regret was highly salient for her. While she thought it was unfair to take the money out of the South African economy, ultimately it was the anticipated regret of speaking to her son about a potential scandal that led her to report the issue. As she says:

> What's he going to ask me when he's 22? If this turns out to be a scandal, and I transfer the money, and this all blows up…And what might he say to me? Like at 22. He'd say "mom, you were this big, big kahuna there in this company, and it all blew up and you were the treasurer, like, what were you doing?" And really, it was his voice in the future that determined me to pick up the phone and make the call. It was like, I don't want to have that conversation.

The call she made set in motion a series of events that led her to flee to London to escape the threats to her and her family. In London, she was able to find a new job as a treasurer for Virgin Management, but they were trying to purchase LeisureNet so she was dismissed after seven months. Without having worked at the company for at least a year, she had no employment protections for her dismissal. She found it difficult to find employment and ended up destitute and on welfare before slowly rebuilding her life. It eventually took 11 years for the joint CEOs to be convicted and sentenced to seven years in prison. While justice was eventually served, it was a painful road.

Wendy's story illustrates many of the themes mentioned throughout this book. First, her ability to withstand the pressures to conform was partly the result of being an "outsider." Although she socialized with the senior executives, she was not part of the "boys' club." As she says, "I always wanted to be part of the boys' club. But I was never invited to the rugby box. I never went and played golf with them." While being an outsider to the "boys' club" is not a fate she chose, it led her to have greater loyalty to the South Africa people (through not withdrawing funds from the economy) and allowed her to overcome the pressure to conform.

She also wishes she had regulated her emotions more when speaking up, a theme we saw in the chapter on persuasion. She says the request to transfer the money angered her and led her to be aggressive in questioning.

> I'm thundering down the corridor, and I've got all these emotions buzzing in my ear. It's like I felt like a bull with a fly in my ear. And so all the years of frustration, of this resentment of

feeling like a patsy, feeling like a puppet, were rising up inside me....And I remember sort of bursting into the offices of the joint CEOs, and actually kind of really being angry about it. And so my language wasn't measured. My delivering of my questioning was emotionally charged. My emotions leaked out.

Her approach was unproductive. The conversation went nowhere:

They became incredibly defensive. They reminded me of my own vulnerability, I was a single mother. So they reminded me of my own lack of power, my own vulnerability, and they reminded me of their power. And that was the end of the conversation.

The social psychologist Adam Galinsky in his TED talk, "How to Speak Up for Yourself," discusses how we have a "range of acceptable behavior" in any situation.[12] We can be too weak and not speak up when we should or be too aggressive and overstep our bounds. Anger can make us feel powerful and help us speak up. It can also lead us to go too far and overstep our bounds in a way that leads to an unhelpful backlash. Wendy's anger made her feel powerful as she "thundered down the corridors," but she was quickly put in her place. It is not that her anger was unjustified; it just needed to be appropriately channeled.

Rather than being forceful and emotionally charged, if she could replay her actions, she would aim to "induce a conversation" rather than demand an outcome of the conversation itself. As she says, "How do you frame the conversation so that you're investing in just inducing the conversation and not necessary in the outcome of the conversation itself?" By taking a different stance, you can lower the stakes of the conversation and not aim for immediate acceptance of your viewpoint. This allows the other party to think through your viewpoint and perhaps change course. It's no guarantee of success, but it avoids the backfire effect of defensiveness.

Surprisingly, Wendy says she regrets not speaking up earlier at LeisureNet. She says that there was a pattern of "lawful but awful" behavior that began with the practice of a "scoresheet" where senior executives could purchase items through the company and have it deducted from their income to reduce their taxes. At first, this was for small items, such as stationery for their children, but in one meeting there appeared a listing for 10,000 pounds for crystal crockery by the CEOs. As Wendy recalls, "I remember distinctly looking sideways around the table: *Did anybody else notice the 10,000 pounds?* And nobody said anything." Others had noticed it but kept silent. In the corridors after the meeting, we were all saying, "Hey, guys, did you just see that? 10,000 pounds? Like what's the deal there?" This practice of invoicing personal expenses through the company began to escalate:

> The second month went by and that crystal crockery had transformed into big vehicles, private cars bought for their children. So we're talking Range Rovers, Porsches, Mercedes Benz cars. And these were on the Excel spreadsheet. And once again, here's a second opportunity for one of us, we were all professionally qualified individuals, did one of us…actually say, what's the deal? Again, we just said nothing, but we all gossiped in the corridors.

This practice continued and eventually led to the purchase and renovation of large homes, all completed through the company's finances to avoid personal income tax. For Wendy—who would eventually blow the whistle and pay a great personal cost for doing so—she regrets not doing more about this early "lawful but awful" behavior. As she says:

> When I look back on, I think to myself, I had so many opportunities to say something, and yet I chose like my peer group, who are all very good people. We all were, as I say, professional, qualified professional people. And we all chose to remain silent. And nobody really measured our sort of moral competence. We were technically competent, but how morally competent were we really? I do really believe, and I look back at it through the lens of regret, because I do believe that if I had said something, it could have changed, at least it would have been, it would have induced conversation. And it could have, might have changed the trajectory of the incrementalization of these sorts of "lawful but awful" behaviors that became illegal behaviors. And so eventually, I believe, looking back, that we all gave them tacit permission to escalate their wrongdoing, because we just did nothing.

Here we see wistful regret, as Wendy's *inaction* is hard to justify and explain to herself. She has distance from the situation and has become a different person, making her inaction hard to justify.

We also see the shifting of norms—in small increments—which changes our perception of what is acceptable. The process has been labeled the "normalization of corruption" or the "slippery slope effect" in ethical judgments.[13] At its most basic, the "slippery slope" is rationalizing small shifts in unethical behavior. For example: It's *just* 10,000 pounds for crystal crockery. I'm sure they need it to impress clients. Or, if we don't have perks like the ability to purchase cars, they can go to another company that would have those perks. These slow shifts alter one's perception of what is allowable. For Wendy, the transfer of funds that she reported crossed over a bright line of illegal behavior, but she regrets not questioning the pattern of behavior that preceded it.

Researchers have found that inducing a "prevention focus" or thinking long term about negative consequences can help overcome the slippery slope effect.[14] This was partly true of Wendy's experience as she thought about the money transfer leading to a scandal and her role in it. She imagined it was going to "blow up" and didn't want to be complicit, especially in the eyes of her son. But she didn't thwart the slippery slope at smaller infractions. It can be a burdensome task and thwarting small infractions can make us seem moralistic, rigid, and alarmist. In Wendy's case, she might have spoken up about the crystal crockery and done so in a way that "induced a conversation" rather than demand the practice be stopped. She might have asked questions such as "Is it right to avoid our income taxes for these personal expenses? Is there a limit we should place on this?" Instead, everyone's silence offered tacit permission of the practice and it continued unchecked. This may unfairly shift the burden of stopping unethical practices on those with less power, but the alternative is to "go along."

It's reasonable to ask ourselves if we would have spoken up in a similar scenario to Wendy's. As you would assume, most of us believe we would. In an experiment testing whether participants disobey or blow the whistle, researchers created a fictional scenario (unbeknownst to participants) asking them to write a letter of support for a "sensory deprivation study." Participants were told that the experiment had already been conducted by a colleague in another country and that "All of those people panicked, their cognitive abilities were impaired temporarily, some experienced visual and auditory hallucinations."[15] Nevertheless, the researcher wanted to investigate "the effects of sensory deprivation on brain function." Participants were left in a room and could either (1) write a letter in support of the research, (2) refuse to write the letter, or (3) anonymously submit a letter to the research committee in a mailbox (i.e., blow the whistle). How many would refuse to write the letter or blow the whistle? Of the 149 participants, only 14 percent refused, and 9 percent blew the whistle. It's hard to know if these numbers are objectively low. Would the "sensory deprivation study" seem valid to most people? The researchers also gave the scenario to a separate group of participants and asked what they believed participants would do. In this sample, 32 percent believed participants would refuse and 64 percent thought participants would blow the whistle—a large disparity from reality.[16] We are aware that situations are powerful but tend to underestimate how powerful.

Wendy says that 14 years after she blew the whistle and the CEOs went to jail, she received an e-mail from a fellow employee at LeisureNet. The individual said, "I knew everything that you knew." However, "…the system of incentives. I had just bought a house, my son was going to private school, even mentioned his kitchen cupboards." He said, "I was far too invested in that…I live with the shame and regret today. And I just want to kind of redeem myself from that." Here we see an individual, with the same information as Wendy, who didn't speak up. He had a lot to lose, as many of us do. This individual had awareness of the situation, yet chose to do nothing and he lives with the "regret" today, which further supports the notion that we most regret our *inactions*.

Ethicists have also examined the cases where we sense there may be unethical action but aren't sure and just move on.[17] In some sense, we are motivated to be unaware. Max Bazerman, a professor at Harvard Business School, describes a mindset of "Life is busy, I don't know who to report this information to, I'm not positive that something's wrong—I just *feel* that something's wrong."[18] Bazerman himself had experienced not taking action when in 2005 he was to testify against a tobacco company and asked by a government attorney to water down his testimony. The prosecution eventually lowered the fine it was seeking from $130 million to $10 million, and in the newspapers another expert witness disclosed an attempt to get him to water down his recommendations. After learning about this witness-tampering, Bazerman went public with his own story, "but his initial passivity haunts him: why didn't he say anything?"[19]

Our level of awareness falls along a continuum, from intentional complicity (knowing a law is being broken) to a sense that something isn't right but not exploring an issue further because of where it might lead. Of course, many things become clear in hindsight: What were vague signals in the moment become flashing red signals in retrospect. Organizational psychologists describe being more *mindful* of cues in the present that may lead to disasters in the future (i.e., a "prevention focus").[20] Being more mindful has been found as a key performance indicator for high-reliability organizations, such as hospitals and aircraft carriers. In these contexts, not speaking up can lead to catastrophe and loss of life. Individuals need to be vigilant about how small cues can be the precursor to catastrophe. In other organizations, the potential outcomes may not be as vivid, but not speaking up still can have dramatic consequences, not the least of which is regret for not speaking up and taking action.

Ultimately, Wendy's courageousness was recognized by her son. As she was in the "spin dryer" early on in the backlash, her son said she was his "hero." At present, Wendy is hopeful that the current trend of employee activism is more powerful than a lone whistleblower taking action. Instead, in groups, you can harness the power of social forces. This can mitigate the risk of being ostracized and dismissed as a lone individual against a giant corporation.

Wendy's story can teach us many things, including the support needed to help whistleblowers, but it also attunes us to "anticipated regret." We should ask what this sense of regret is signaling to us, how our current actions might be viewed in the future, and how we might be deviating from our sense of right and wrong. These are very important questions, but if we don't have a sense of self-efficacy that we can bring about positive results, we won't take action.

Self-Efficacy and the Road Ahead

It is my hope that this book has increased your sense of self-efficacy in speaking up as an independent thinker. Self-efficacy is a belief that you can bring about the desired results you have for your work and life—that you are able to persevere and face challenges.[21] Research on self-efficacy was pioneered by Albert Bandura of Stanford University, one of the most influential psychologists of the past 100 years. One of his earliest studies examined the incremental process of overcoming phobias, in one case the fear of snakes.[22] It serves as a useful metaphor for the process of overcoming fear in speaking up.

To see how one's self-efficacy can be enhanced, Bandura used a process called "guided mastery." Guided mastery is a facilitated process of taking small incremental steps that are just beyond one's current capabilities. They take a person from a belief that "I can't" to "I can!" In Bandura's study conducted in the early 1970s, he began with a snake phobic being in a building with a snake in the next room. Participants were told they'd be going into the room with the snake, to which they responded with recognizable trepidation and resistance. Importantly, these individuals had joined this study because they wanted to make a change. Their lives were being negatively impacted by the phobia, which included intrusive thoughts and nightmares about snakes. This illustrates the important precondition of having a motivation to change.

After overcoming the trepidation of being in a room next to a snake, Bandura then had a trained facilitator take them through a series of steps. It started with just looking at the snake (a boa constrictor) through a one-way mirror. The steps progressed to entering the room, then touching it with a finger, holding it (sometimes aided by initially wearing a glove), and then having their hand out as the snake moved forward. It progressed to having the snake crawl about the room and retrieving it and letting it lie around their neck and lap. These steps were inconceivable to the participants just a few hours prior. It took individuals varying amounts of time to slowly make it through these steps, with some individuals completing them in 40 minutes and others taking 7 hours, with an average of 90 minutes. It was a remarkable transformation, taking individuals with an extreme phobia to confronting and overcoming their fear.

You might argue, however, that self-efficacy is highly domain specific—that you believe in your abilities in some domains and not others. While this is certainly true, in Bandura's research on snake phobics, he found a *generalized* increase in self-efficacy among partici-pants. As one participant stated, "As a result of feeling more confident and in charge of myself I can manage other fears…I have a greater self-confidence. When something comes up that is new or unknown to me I feel, 'Well, I can handle that.'"[23] Bandura further noted in a follow-up interview that participants began tackling and overcoming nonrelated fears, such as public speaking, horseback riding, or exploring new aspects of their job.[24] This is one of the most heartening findings of the study—that conquering our fears in one domain can increase our sense of confidence that we can tackle challenges in another. This is espe-cially true if we have learned a *process* of change, of learning to regulate our fear in a way that is applicable in other pursuits.

As mentioned, these individuals joined this experiment because their lives were being negatively impacted by their snake phobia; they had a motivation to change. It was a motivation to change that moved beyond ambivalence—of simultaneously wanting and *not* wanting something. In many instances, we desire to have our voice heard but do not want the blowback and stress that will ensue. It is like we are driving a car and have "one foot on the gas and one foot on the brake."[25] We want to speak up but also want harmony and to be considered a "team player." We need to recognize, however, if we are "braking" too much—if we are self-censoring too much. If Bandura's snake phobics teach us anything, it is the value of facing our fears and doing so incrementally, if possible, for it leads to a heightened sense of generalized self-efficacy in meeting the challenges of work and life.

In addition to guided mastery experiences, there are many ways to improve your sense of self-efficacy, including vicarious learning, social support, and lowering your physiological arousal (i.e., not being in an overly stressed state). First, it is my hope that reading the stories and ideas in this book has been the foundation for creating your own mastery experiences—taking incremental steps that slowly promote self-efficacy and temper fears. This might be in speaking up in situations with lower stakes or in aiming to just "induce a conversation," as Wendy Addison mentioned, rather than aiming for immediate acceptance of your ideas. Or you can aim for more indirect ways of testing your ideas, as we saw in Chapter 3, such as asking questions and "what if?" Much like Bandura's snake phobics, this gradual process can help you become more comfortable raising difficult issues.

Throughout the stories of this book, I hope you have also experienced vicarious learning. You've been able to learn from the experiences of others and see the pitfalls, high points, and lessons learned. This was another insight from Bandura in his description of social learning.[26] We can learn by watching others and modeling their behavior. This is at once obvious, but also profound. You don't have to learn everything through personal experience and failure. You can learn vicariously through others to help guide your way. Researchers have found that having leaders in your organization model speaking up supports voice self-efficacy.[27] This was particularly true for gender congruent expressions of voice, for example, a woman seeing a female leader in her organization express a viewpoint. We learn vicariously through their experiences, and it increases our sense of efficacy that we can do the same. This highlights the importance of role models and how they serve as an inspirational source of self-efficacy (i.e., "if they can do it, so can I").

Social support, or as Bandura labels it "verbal persuasion," is another means of increasing your sense of efficacy. This may occur in receiving credible encouragement of your personal capabilities from another. This is another reason to seek out mentors and coaches to help encourage you along the way, in addition to family and friends. Finally, our sense of efficacy and willingness to act are a result of our physiological stress levels. If you've ever been overwhelmed (who hasn't?), your sense of efficacy in situations is dampened. This highlights that while self-efficacy can be stable, it does have a transient quality given the current demands we are facing. It is another reason to invest in stress reduction activities such as mindfulness as a means of helping us reach our goals.[28]

These four sources of self-efficacy are helpful to keep in mind as you think about speaking up and leading change. By and large, they are likely to be implicit factors—background determinants impacting your belief in your abilities. But, you can more explicitly consider ways of boosting your sense of self-efficacy: What guided mastery experiences can you engage in to incrementally help you lead change? How can you continue to vicariously learn from the experiences of others? What social support and encouragement do you need? And how can you manage stress and overwhelm?

While self-efficacy is important, our context also matters a great deal. We need organizations and managers that provide a moderate level of psychological safety and openness to new ideas. Psychological safety is a perception that we won't be unduly punished for taking reasonable risks. It is measured by asking whether you are able to bring up problems and tough issues.[29] Our sense of self-efficacy in any situation would be a combination of a belief in our capabilities and the justified constraints of our environment, including whether there is psychological safety. Thus, while our self-beliefs are important, our environment matters. As Bandura states, "The exercise of personal agency over the direction one's life takes varies depending on the nature and modifiability of the environment. The environment is not a monolith bearing down on individuals unidirectionally."[30] Our environments, as Bandura states, are imposed, selected, and created. There are relatively objective aspects of our environments that are *imposed* upon us (e.g., economic conditions), we also *select* what aspects of the environment to attend to (e.g., "senior leadership didn't support that idea several years ago"), and we also construct and *create* our environments (e.g., "senior leadership won't support anything I say"). We obviously hold greater agency in how we select and create our environments, without forgetting that there are relatively objective aspects that are imposed upon us.

Another useful distinction in self-efficacy research is whether we have confidence in our tools and tactics. This distinguishes between *internal* efficacy and *means* efficacy. As Dov Eden, a researcher in the field, states:

> Just as a high level of internal efficacy produces high performance expectations, spurs effort, and thereby enhances performance, so a high level of means efficacy makes one expect success and impels one to use the valued means energetically, culminating in improved performance: "Wow! With a mitt like this, I'll catch any ball coming at me!"[31]

Earlier chapters explored specific tools and tactics that can boost your level of means efficacy, whether it is asking question such as "'what if?' rather than more direct challenges that put people on the defensive or using persuasion tactics such as social proof or highlighting inconsistencies between an organization's values and current practices. In Chapter 4, we also saw key tactics to lead a process of change, such as involving others through discovery and taking an experimental approach. And in Chapter 5, we saw many processes you can use on your team to create an environment where individuals share their thoughts and perspectives, such as setting the norm to ask "Is it true?" to spur critical debate. If you've got specific tactics and methods, it can increase your sense of means efficacy that you can handle the challenges you'll face.

These are mainly *cognitive* tools. They are considerations that can help you take more effective action, and the more tools you have the more effectively you can handle situations, using the appropriate tactic given the situation. You will not always be confident in your abilities (and face challenges along the way), but you can remember the experiences and tools throughout this book to help you speak up and lead positive change in your organization.

Notes

Chapter 1

1. March (1991).
2. Participants were recruited for interviews from personal networks based on their willingness to discuss their experience of having an independent point of view in the workplace. Using the critical incident technique (Flanagan 1954), participants described their experiences in depth. The incidents primarily occurred within the United States.
3. Independent thinking is closely related to employee voice; however, independent thinking is a broader term than employee voice and refers to independence with respect to an immediate reference group. Employee voice is a form of independent thinking within an organizational context. Independent thinking, however, can be in reference to any group, be it a political party, a mainstream cultural assumption (e.g., housing prices always go up!), or any social group. I will use the terms independent thinking and employee voice interchangeably throughout the book, as they are highly overlapping constructs, with the main difference being that employee voice has an implied context.
4. Except where permission was given, all names are pseudonyms and identifying details of an interviewee's story have been removed.
5. Jacobs (2017), p. 37.
6. To some theorists, the social aspect of thinking does not rely on the physical presence of others (Blumer 1969; Weick 1995). We can think through what others might say or do in our current situation. While this is certainly true, the notion that all thinking is social is meant to keep us from simplistically ignoring the role of culture and social interaction (Weick 1995). Our thinking is intimately intertwined with the cultural worlds in which we inhabit and have inhabited. By describing independent thinking, I work to avoid this blind spot of ignoring the origins of our perspectives. Nevertheless, the term "independent thinking" is meant to describe a point of view that is independent with respect to our current reference group. And, in some situations, the role of culture and social interaction in thinking might be minimal: for example, in putting together a puzzle never built before, such as analyzing the risk of mortgage-backed securities ahead of the financial crisis of 2008 (Lewis 2010), or, in more distant times, Copernicus' calculations

that the earth was revolving around the sun. In many cases, the mind isn't simply a cultural vessel, but instead actively creating new knowledge. Thus, while thinking may rely on the remembered perspectives of others, by independent thinking, I am referring to a point of view that is independent of the traditions and norms of our current context.

7. Asch (1956), p. 7.
8. Ibid, p. 28.
9. Ibid.
10. Ibid, p. 31.
11. Ibid.
12. Ibid, p. 40.
13. Kegan and Lahey (2009).
14. Asch (1956), p. 45.
15. Asch was writing before Rosenberg's (1965) seminal work on self-esteem. Personal worth and self-esteem can be considered synonymous.
16. Deutsch and Gerard (1955).
17. Berns et al. (2005).
18. Specifically, the baseline error rate for participants was 13.8 percent which increased to 41 percent when the group gave an incorrect response (Berns et al. 2005).
19. Berns (2008).
20. Nemeth (2018).
21. While many of these safeguards were kept in place, as Cheryl and others left the board, several of them were rolled back. This was dissatisfying for Cheryl to hear; nevertheless, the school was more protected financially than if she had conformed from the start.
22. Schwartz et al. (2012), p. 664.
23. Rohan (2000).
24. Klaczynski and Lavallee (2005), p. 4.
25. Kuhn, Cheney, and Weinstock (2000).
26. Hewstone and Martin (2010).
27. Liang, Farh, and Farh (2012).

Chapter 2

1. Burry was profiled in a bestselling book on the financial crisis by Michael Lewis, and the actor Christian Bale played Burry in the movie adaptation of *The Big Short*.
2. Jacoby and Rudavsky (2011).
3. Burry (2011).
4. Lewis (2010), p. 31.
5. Burry (2010).

6. Lewis (2010).
7. Ibid, p. 187.
8. Lewis (2010).
9. Courtney (2010).
10. Burry (2011).
11. Abrami et al. (2015).
12. Willingham (2007).
13. Pauling (1990), p. 63.
14. For additional work on variation and selection models of creativity, see Campbell (1960), Simonton (2011), or Weick (1989).
15. Kahneman (2011), p. 97.
16. Sanchez and Dunning (2018).
17. Grant (2021).
18. Dunning (2011).
19. Dane (2010).
20. Ibid, p. 579.
21. Dane (2010).
22. Hargadon (2006), p. 202.
23. The T-shaped image is widely used by companies, notably McKinsey & Company, to describe the aspiration of wanting both breadth and depth of experience and expertise.
24. Cohen and Prusak (2001), p. 15.
25. Simonton (1995), p. 481.
26. Kounios and Beeman (2014).
27. Johnson (2010), p. 77.
28. Thaler (2015a), p. 40.
29. Thaler and Benartzi (2004).
30. This section is partly based on a blog I published titled "Slow Hunches, Curiosity, and Innovative Ideas" on *Psychology Today*.
31. Thaler (2015a), p. 22.
32. Litman (2008); Loewenstein (1994); Von Stumm, Hell, and Chamorro-Premuzic (2011).
33. Thaler (2015a), p. 40.
34. Thaler (1987).
35. Thaler (2015b).
36. Thaler (2017).
37. Watkins (2015).
38. Ibid.
39. Frey (2002).
40. Asch (1956).
41. Watkins (2015).
42. Carozza (2007).

43. See Gibson and Vermeulen (2003).

44. Steven is Asian and this story takes place in an Asian country.

45. Stanovich (2008).

46. Chen, Shechter, and Chaiken (1996).

47. This depiction of science as the pursuit of truth is certainly open to claims of naïveté by philosophers of science, but as Harvard linguist and psychologist Steven Pinker (2018) states, "Many historians of science consider it naïve to treat science as the pursuit of true explanations of the world. The result is like a report of a basketball game by a dance critic who is not allowed to say that the players are trying to throw the ball through the hoop" (p. 396).

48. Italics in original, McIntyre (2019), p. 7.

49. Pinker (2018), p. 392.

50. Stanovich (2008).

51. Baron and Spranca (1997).

52. Ibid.

53. See the 2017 film *Shock and Awe* that recounts the efforts of Knight Ridder journalists and their reporting of the lead up to the Iraq invasion. This section is also partly based on a blog I published titled "Seeing Through Groupthink" on *Psychology Today*.

54. Follmer (2008).

55. Abcarian (2013).

56. Moyers (2007).

57. Ibid.

58. Landay (2002).

59. Wemple (2013).

60. From the editors; The *Times* and Iraq (2004).

61. Massing (2004).

62. Knight Ridder Newspapers (2004).

63. Sheldon (2004).

64. Festinger (1957).

65. Vadera, Pratt, and Mishra (2013), p. 1223.

66. You might argue that being "constructively deviant" is about making an appeal to improve organizational performance. However, Warren (2003) describes how appeals to organizational performance aren't synonymous with appeals to hypernorms, stating: "In my conceptualization, behavior that does not align with organizational performance but conforms to hypernorms (as seen in the example of disobeying orders to dump toxic waste) is constructive or helpful to society, even though in past research scholars may have deemed the behavior destructive, using organizational performance as a normative standard" (p. 625).

67. Donaldson and Dunfee (1999); Warren (2003).

Chapter 3

1. Geddes and Callister (2007); Callister, Geddes, and Gibson (2017).
2. Gross (2015), pp. 4–5.
3. Seery, Gabriel, Lupien, and Shimuzu (2016).
4. Blascovich (2008).
5. MacCann and Roberts (2008).
6. Grant (2013).
7. Cialdini (2009).
8. Nyhan and Reifler (2010).
9. Pinker, Nowak, and Lee (2008).
10. Lam, Lee, and Sui (2019).
11. One simple phrasing that can vary the directness of one's message is using the inclusive pronoun "we" rather than "you." For example, "we should consider," rather than "you should consider" [See Lam, Lee, and Sui (2019)].
12. Lam, Lee, and Sui (2019).
13. Tetlock and Gardner (2015), p. 162.
14. Burris (2022), p. 140.
15. Fast, Burris, and Bartel (2014).
16. Mueller (2019).
17. Grant (2021); Miller and Moyers (2017); Miller and Rollnick (2012).
18. Kotter and Cohen (2002), p. 2.
19. Schroeder, Kardas, and Epley (2017).
20. Cialdini (2009), p. 99.
21. DiMaggio and Powell (1983).
22. Cooperrider and Whitney (2001).
23. Cialdini (2009).
24. Kelly and Medina (2014).
25. Grant (2020).
26. O'Keefe (2016).
27. Crano (2010).
28. Satterstrom, Kerrissey, and DiBenigno (2021).

Chapter 4

1. Heifetz, Grashow, and Linsky (2009).
2. Heifetz and Linsky (2002), p. 68.
3. Pickel (1995); Wolf and Montgomery (1977).
4. Brehm and Brehm (1981).
5. Grant (2021).
6. Church and Samuelson (2017); Smerek (2017).

7. Oreg and Berson (2019).

8. Gibbons (2015), p. 30.

9. Rodgers (2003).

10. Ibid, pp. 310–311.

11. Ford, Ford, and D'Amelio (2008), p. 362.

12. Gladwell (2000); Rodgers (2003).

13. Kotter (2012).

14. Ibid.

15. Of course, categorizing any initiative a "failure" requires nuance (e.g.. Over what time period? And by what metrics?). Some cases are nonambiguous (e.g., shutting down an initiative), but many initiatives may marginally continue with limited results. For the original 70 percent failure statistic, see Beer and Nohria (2000). For counterarguments to the 70 percent "myth," see Gibbons (2015) and Hughes (2011).

16. Brown (2009); Burnes (2004); Heath and Heath (2010); Schein (2017); Stouten, Rousseau, and De Cremer (2018); Weick and Quinn (1999).

17. Kahneman (2011), p. 97.

18. Smerek (2017).

19. For a review of helping practitioners "tell stories," see Crandall, Klein, and Hofmann (2006) or Torres (2021).

20. For "unfreezing," see the work of Kurt Levin; for "creating a sense of urgency," see Kotter (2012); and for "learning anxiety," see Schein (2017).

21. Camerer, Loewenstein, and Weber (1989).

22. Grant (2022); see also Duarte (2010).

23. Baum and Dahlin (2007).

24. Staw, Sandelands, and Dutton (1981). During a crisis, there can also be centralization of control, such that lower levels in the organization feel powerless to act (further leading to "threat rigidity").

25. Weick (1984); Sitkin (1992).

26. Kotter (1995).

27. Weick (1984), p. 47.

28. Sitkin (1992), p. 238.

29. Sunstein and Hastie (2015), p. 10.

Chapter 5

1. Dalio (2017), p. 532.

2. Burnes and Cooke (2012).

3. Lewin, Lippitt, and White (1939), p. 271.

4. Gastil (1994a).

5. Harms et al. (2018); White and Lippitt (1960).

6. Gastil (1994a), p. 402.

7. Ibid, p. 403.

8. Harms et al. (2018).

9. Dalio (2017), p. 32.

10. Ibid, p. 34.

11. Harms et al. (2018).

12. McFarlin and Sweeney (1996); Tyler, Rasinski, and Spodick (1985).

13. Tyler, Degoey, and Smith (1996).

14. Brockner and Wisenfeld (1996); see also Heath and Heath (2013).

15. Brockner and Wisenfeld (1996), p. 206.

16. For a portrait of Google as such a fractious environment, see Tiku (2019).

17. Nadella, Shaw, and Nichols (2017), pp. 8081.

18. Hofstede, Hofstede, and Minkov (2010), p. 61.

19. Ibid.

20. Earley and Erez (1997), p. 179.

21. Hofstede, Hofstede, and Minkov (2010).

22. History.com Editors (2019).

23. Janis (1982), p. 9.

24. Doublethink has various connotations in George Orwell's book *1984*. They involve how a totalitarian government will aim to obscure truth by making two claims that are contradictory, for example, "war is peace" or "freedom is slavery."

25. Janis (1982), p. 9.

26. Esser (1998).

27. Harvey (1974).

28. Ibid, pp. 6566.

29. Westphal and Bednar (2005), p. 286.

30. Nemeth (2018); Park (2000).

31. Dalio (2017), p. 187.

32. For additional items, see Stanovich et al. (2016), p. 366; see also Stanovich and West (1997).

33. Quinn and Schlenker (2002).

34. Chen, Schechter, and Chaiken (1996).

35. Lerner and Tetlock (1999).

36. Quinn and Schlenker (2002), pp. 481482.

37. Dalio (2017).

38. Horwich (2013); or Michael Patrick Lynch's TED Talk "How to see past your own perspective and find truth."

39. Thompson (2003); Van de Ven and Delbecq (1971).

40. For a meta-analysis on how a devil's advocate can improve decision making, see Schwenk (1990). Ironically, there is dissent about the effectiveness of a devil's advocate. Charlan Nemeth (2018), in particular, argues that, especially in lab settings, when a devil's advocate seems highly inauthentic and their dissent seems contrived, it is largely ineffective.

41. Tsai and Bendersky (2016), p. 148; Weingart et al. (2015).

Chapter 6

1. The actual location of the office has been removed for confidentiality reasons. However, I use "New York" for readability.

2. In research on circumvention (i.e., going around your boss to speak to someone higher in the organization), 81 accounts from full-time employees were coded for the relationship outcome that occurred between the subordinate and superior who was circumvented (Kassing 2007). In half of the accounts, it led to a deterioration of the superior/subordinate relationship, with the other outcomes including "compromise" (n=11), "development" of the relationship based on gratitude for circumvention when it led to a positive outcome for the supervisor (n=10), "understanding" when supervisors realized they initially handled the issue poorly (n=9), and "neutrality" with no change in the relationship (n=10). This highlights that while circumvention is a risky strategy, it can lead to positive outcomes.

3. Zeelenberg (1999), p. 326.

4. Gilovich, Medvec, and Kahneman (1998).

5. Crucially, the action (or inaction) would have been behavior that deviated from what is socially appropriate in a situation, such that our behavior is hard to justify (see Feldman 2020). While deviating from what is "normal" is crucial to the experience of regret, I am primarily concerned, however, with long-term regret (i.e., wistful regret) and the implications for action based on its experience.

6. Gilbert (2006); Gilovich and Medvec (1995).

7. Gilovich and Medvic (1995), p. 388.

8. Gilbert (2006), p. 179.

9. Gilovich and Medvic (1995), p. 390.

10. Wendy Addison's story and quotations are compiled from a personal interview and published interviews (Addison 2018).

11. Addison (2018).

12. Galinsky (2016).

13. Ashforth and Anand (2003); Gino and Bazerman (2009); Welsh, Ordóñez, Snyder, and Christian (2015).

14. Gino and Margolis (2011).

15. Bocchiaro, Zimbardo, and Van Lange (2021), p. 38.
16. Ibid.
17. Bazerman and Tenbrunsel (2011).
18. Nguyen (2014), p. 11.
19. Ibid, p. 12.
20. Weick and Sutcliffe (2007).
21. Bandura (1997).
22. Bandura, Adams, and Beyer (1977).
23. Bandura et al. (1977), p. 136.
24. Kelley and Kelley (2013).
25. Kegan and Lahey (2009), p. 60.
26. Bandura (2005).
27. Yan, Tangirala, Vadera, and Ekkirala (2022).
28. Kabat-Zinn (1990).
29. Edmondson (1999).
30. Bandura (2005), p. 18.
31. Eden, Ganzach, Flumin-Granat, and Zigman (2010), p. 689.

References

Abcarian, R. March 19, 2013. "Iraq War 10th Anniversary: A Dark Mark for News Media." *Los Angeles Times*. https://latimesblogs.latimes.com/lanow/2013/03/iraq-war-anniversary-a-dark-mark-for-the-news-media.html.

Abrami, P.C., R.M. Bernard, E. Borokhovski, D.I. Waddington, C.A. Wade, and T. Persson. 2015. "Strategies for Teaching Students to Think Critically: A Meta-Analysis." *Review of Educational Research* 85, no. 2, pp. 275–314.

Addison, W. 2018. *ETHIC Intelligence*. www.youtube.com/watch?v=SgoBrOM8OA4.

Asch, S.E. 1956. "Studies of Independence and Conformity. A Minority of One Against a Unanimous Majority." *Psychological Monographs* 70, no. 9, pp. 1–70.

Ashforth, B.E. and V. Anand. 2003. "The Normalization of Corruption in Organizations." *Research in Organizational Behavior* 25, pp. 1–52.

Bandura, A. 1997. *Self-Efficacy: The Exercise of Control*. W.H. Freeman.

Bandura, A. 2005. "The Evolution of Social Cognitive Theory." In *Great Minds in Management*, ed. K.G. Smith, pp. 9–35. Oxford University Press.

Bandura, A., N.E. Adams, and J. Beyer. 1977. "Cognitive Processes Mediating Behavioral Changes." *Journal of Personality and Social Psychology* 35, no. 3, pp. 125–139.

Baron, J. and M. Spranca. 1997. "Protected Values." *Organizational Behavior and Human Decision Processes* 70, no. 1, pp. 1–16.

Baum, J.A.C. and K.B. Dahlin. 2007. "Aspiration Performance and Railroads' Patterns of Learning From Train Wrecks and Accidents." *Organization Science* 18, no. 3, pp. 368–385.

Bazerman, M. and A.E. Tenbrunsel. April 2011. "Ethical Breakdowns: Good People often Let Bad Things Happen. Why?" *Harvard Business Review* 89, no. 4, pp. 58–65.

Beer, M. and N. Nohria. 2000. "Cracking the Code of Change." *Harvard Business Review* 78, no. 3, pp. 133–141.

Berns, G.S. 2008. *Iconoclast: A Neuroscientist Reveals How to Think Differently*. Harvard Business School Press.

Berns, G.S., J. Chappelow, C.F. Zink, G. Pagnoni, M.E. Martin-Skurski, and J. Richards. 2005. "Neurobiological Correlates of Social Conformity and Independence During Mental Rotation." *Biological Psychiatry*, 58, pp. 245–253.

Blascovich, J. 2008. "Challenge and Threat." In *Handbook of Approach and Avoidance Motivation*, ed. A.J. Elliot., pp. 431–445. Psychology Press.

Blumer, H. 1969. *Symbolic Interactionism: Perspective and Method.* Prentice Hall.

Bocchiaro, P., P.G. Zimbardo, and P.A.M. Van Lange. 2012. "To Defy of Not to Defy: An Experimental Study of the Dynamics of Disobedience and Whistle-Blowing." *Social Influence* 7, no. 1, pp. 35–50.

Brehm, S.S. and J.W. Brehm. 1981. *Psychological Reactance: A Theory of Freedom and Control.* Academic Press.

Brockner, J. and B.M. Wisenfeld. 1996. "An Integrative Framework for Explaining Reactions to Decisions: Interactive Effects of Outcomes and Procedures." *Psychological Bulletin* 120, pp. 189–208.

Brown, T. 2009. *Change by Design.* HarperCollins.

Burnes, B. 2004. "Kurt Lewin and the Planned Approach to Change: A Re-Appraisal." *Journal of Management Studies* 41, no. 6, pp. 977–1002.

Burnes, B. and B. Cooke. 2012. "The Past, Present and Future of Organization Development: Taking the Long View." *Human Relations* 65, no. 11, pp. 1395–1429.

Burris, E. January–February 2022. "How to Sell Your Ideas up the Chain of Command." *Harvard Business Review*, pp. 139–143.

Burry, M.J. April 3, 2010. "I Saw the Crisis Coming. Why Didn't the Fed?" *The New York Times.* www.nytimes.com/2010/04/04/opinion/04burry.html.

Burry, M.J. April 5, 2011. "Missteps to Mayhem: Inside the Doomsday Machine With the Outsider Who Predicted and Profited From America's Financial Armageddon." Chancellor's Lecture Series at Vanderbilt University. https://news.vanderbilt.edu/2011/04/13/michael-burry-transcript/.

Callister, R.R., D. Geddes, and D.F. Gibson. 2017. "When Is Anger Helpful or Hurtful? Status and Role Impact on Anger Expression and Outcome." *Negotiation and Conflict Management Research* 10, no. 2, pp. 69–87.

Camerer, C., G. Loewenstein, and M. Weber. 1989. "The Curse of Knowledge in Economic Settings: An Experimental Analysis." *The Journal of Political Economy* 97, no. 5, pp. 1232–1254.

Campbell, D.T. 1960. "Blind Variation and Selective Retention in Creative Thought as in Other Knowledge Processes." *Psychological Review* 67, pp. 380–400.

Carozza, D. 2007, January/February. "Interview With Sherron Watkins." *Fraud Magazine.* www.fraud-magazine.com/article.aspx?id=583.

Chen, S., D. Schechter, and S. Chaiken. 1996. "Getting at the Truth or Getting Along: Accuracy- Versus Impression-Motivated Heuristic and Systematic Processing." *Journal of Personality and Social Psychology* 71, no. 2, pp. 262–275.

Church, I.M. and P.L. Samuelson. 2017. *Intellectual Humility: An Introduction to the Philosophy and Science.* Bloomsbury.

Cialdini, R.B. 2009. *Influence: Science and Practice*, 5th ed. Pearson Education.

Cohen, D. and L. Prusak. 2001. *In Good Company: How Social Capital Makes Organizations Work*. Harvard Business School Press.

Cooperrider, D.L. and D. Whitney. 2001. "A Positive Revolution in Change: Appreciative Inquiry." In *Appreciative Inquiry: An Emerging Direction for Organization Development*, eds. D.L. Cooperrider, P.F. Sorensen, T.F. Yaeger, and D. Whitney, pp. 5–29. Stipes Publishing LLC.

Courtney, C. April 5, 2010. "Greenspan, You're Losing the Argument Against Michael Burry, Stop Digging and Stop Acting Like a Fool." *Business Insider*. www.businessinsider.com/greenspan-on-michael-burry-scion-capital-2010-4.

Crandall, B., G. Klein, and R.R. Hoffman. 2006. *Working Minds: A Practitioner's Guide to Cognitive Task Analysis*. MIT Press.

Crano, W.D. 2010. "Majority and Minority Influence in Attitude Formation and Attitude Change: Context/Categorization—Leniency Contract Theory." In *Minority Influence and Innovation: Antecedents, Processes, and Consequences*, eds. M. Hewstone and R. Martin, pp. 60–81. Psychology Press.

Dalio, R. 2017. *Principles: Life and Work*. Simon & Schuster.

Dane, E. 2010. "Reconsidering the Trade-off Between Expertise and Flexibility: A Cognitive Entrenchment Perspective." *Academy of Management Review* 35, no. 4, pp. 579–603.

Deutsch, M. and H.B. Gerard. 1955. "A Study of Normative and Informative Social Influences Upon Individual Judgment." *Journal of Abnormal Social Psychology* 51, pp. 629–636.

DiMaggio, P.J. and W.W. Powell. 1983. "The Iron Cage Revisited: Institutional Isomorphism and Collective Rationality in Organizational Fields." *American Sociological Review* 48, pp. 147–160.

Donaldson, T. and T.W. Dunfee. 1999. "When Ethics Travel: The Promise and Peril of Global Business Ethics." *California Management Review* 41, no. 4, pp. 45–63.

Duarte, N. 2010. *Resonate: Present Visual Stories that Transform Audiences*. John Wiley.

Dunning, D. 2011. "The Dunning-Kruger Effect: On Being Ignorant of One's Own Ignorance." *Advances in Experimental Social Psychology* 44, pp. 247–296.

Earley, P.C. and M. Erez. 1997. *The Transplanted Executive: Why You Need to Understand How Workers in Other Countries See the World Differently*. Oxford University Press.

Eden, D., Y. Ganzach, R. Flumin-Granat, and T. Zigman. 2010. "Augmenting Means Efficacy to Boost Performance: Two Field Experiments." *Journal of Management* 36, pp. 687–713.

Edmondson, A. 1999. "Psychological Safety and Learning in Work Teams." *Administrative Science Quarterly* 44, no. 2, pp. 350–383.

Esser, J.K. 1998. "Alive and Well After 25 Years: A Review of Groupthink Research." *Organizational Behavior and Human Decision Processes* 73, no. 2/3, pp. 116–141.

Fast, N.J., E.R. Burris, and C.A. Bartel. 2014. "Managing to Stay in the Dark: Managerial Self-Efficacy, Ego Defensiveness, and the Aversion to Employee Voice." *Academy of Management Journal* 57, no. 4, pp. 1013–1034.

Feldman, G. 2020. "What Is Normal? Dimensions of Action-Inaction Normality and Their Impact on Regret in the Action-Effect." *Cognition and Emotion* 34, no. 4, pp. 728–742.

Festinger, L. 1957. *A Theory of Cognitive Dissonance.* Stanford University Press.

Flanagan, J.C. 1954. "The Critical Incident Technique." *Psychological Bulletin* 51, no. 4, pp. 327–358.

Follmer, M. March 28, 2008. "The Reporting Team that Got Iraq Right." *The Huffington Post.* www.huffpost.com/entry/the-reporting-team-that-g_n_91981.

Ford, J.D., L.W. Ford, and A. D'Amelio. 2008. "Resistance to Change: The Rest of the Story." *Academy of Management Review* 33, pp. 362–377.

Frey, J. January 25, 2002. "The Woman Who Saw Red; Enron Whistle-Blower Sherron Watkins Warned of the Trouble to Come." *The Washington Post.*

Galinsky, A.D. 2016. "How to Speak Up for Yourself." *TED Talk.* www.ted.com/talks/adam_galinsky_how_to_speak_up_for_yourself.

Gastil, J. 1994a. "A Meta-Analytic Review of the Productivity and Satisfaction of Democratic and Autocratic Leadership." *Small Group Research* 25, no. 3, pp. 384–410.

Gastil, J. 1994b. "A Definition and Illustration of Democratic Leadership." *Human Relations* 47, no. 8, pp. 953–975.

Geddes, D. and R.R. Callister. 2007. "Crossing the Line(s): A Dual Threshold Model of Anger in Organizations." *Academy of Management Review* 32, no. 3, pp. 721–746.

Gibbons, P. 2015. *The Science of Successful Organizational Change: How Leaders Set Strategy, Change Behavior, and Create an Agile Culture.* Pearson Education.

Gibson, C. and F. Vermeulen. 2003. "A Healthy Divide: Subgroups as a Stimulus for Team Learning Behavior." *Administrative Science Quarterly* 48, no. 2, pp. 202–239.

Gilbert, D.T. 2006. *Stumbling on Happiness.* Alfred Knopf.

Gilovich, T. and V.H. Medvec. 1995. "The experience of Regret: What, When, and Why." *Psychological Review* 102, no. 2, pp. 379–395.

Gilovich, T., V.H. Medvec, and D. Kahneman. 1998. "Varieties of Regret: A Debate and Partial Resolution." *Psychological Review* 105, no. 3, pp. 602–605.

Gino, F. and M.H. Bazerman. 2009. "When Misconduct Goes Unnoticed: The Acceptability of Gradual Erosion of Others' Unethical Behavior." *Journal of Experimental Social Psychology* 45, pp. 708–719.

Gino, F. and J.D. Margolis. 2011. "Bringing Ethics into Focus: How Regulatory Focus and Risk Preferences Influence (Un)ethical Behavior." *Organizational Behavior and Human Decision Processes* 115, pp. 145–156.

Gladwell, M. 2000. *The Tipping Point: How Little Things Can Make a Big Difference.* Little, Brown and Company.

Grant, A.M. 2013. "Rocking the Boat but Keeping It Steady: The Role of Emotion Regulation in Employee Voice." *Academy of Management Journal* 56, no. 6, pp. 1703–1723.

Grant, A.M. 2020. "Authenticity is a Double-Edged Sword." *Worklife.* [Audio Podcast]. www.adamgrant.net/podcast/.

Grant, A.M. 2021. *Think Again: The Power of Knowing What You Don't Know.* Viking.

Grant, A.M. 2022. "How to Pitch Your Best Ideas." *Worklife.* [Audio Podcast]. www.adamgrant.net/podcast/.

Gross, J.J. 2015. "Emotion Regulation: Current Status and Future Prospects." *Psychological Inquiry* 26, pp. 1–26.

Hargadon, A.B. 2006. "Bridging Old Worlds and Building New Ones: Toward a Microsociology of Creativity." In *Creativity and Innovation in Organizational Teams*, eds. L.L. Thompson and H.-S. Choi, pp. 199–216. Lawrence Erlbaum Associates.

Harms, P. D., D. Wood, K. Landay, P.B. Lester, and G. Vogelgesang Lester. 2018. "Autocratic Leaders and Authoritarian Followers Revisited: A Review and Agenda for the Future." *Leadership Quarterly* 29, pp. 105–122.

Harvey, J.B. 1974. "The Abilene Paradox: The Management of Agreement." *Organizational Dynamics* 3, no. 1, pp. 63–80.

Heath, C. and D. Heath. 2010. *Switch: How to Change Things When Change Is Hard.* Random House.

Heath, C. and D. Heath. 2013. *Decisive: How to Make Better Choices in Life and Work.* Random House.

Heifetz, R.A., A. Grashow, and M. Linsky. 2009. *The Practice of Adaptive Leadership: Tools and Tactics for Changing Your Organization and the World.* Harvard Business Press.

Heifetz, R.A. and M. Linsky. 2002. "A Survival Guide for Leaders." *Harvard Business Review* 80, no. 6, pp. 65–74.

Hewstone, M. and R. Martin. 2010. "Minority Influence: From Groups to Attitudes and Back Again." In *Minority Influence and Innovation: Antecedents, Processes, and Consequences*, eds. M. Hewstone and R. Martin, pp. 307–330. Psychology Press.

History.com Editors. 2019. *Bay of Pigs Invasion.* A&E Television Networks. www.history.com/topics/cold-war/bay-of-pigs-invasion (accessed October 23, 2019).

Hofstede, G.H., G.J. Hofstede, and M. Minkov. 2010. *Cultures and Organizations*: *Software of the Mind: Intercultural Cooperation and Its Importance for Survival*, 3rd ed. McGraw-Hill.

Horwich, P. March 3, 2013. "Was Wittgenstein right?" *The New York Times*.

Hughes, M. 2011. "Do 70 Percent of All Organizational Change Initiatives Really Fail?" *Journal of Change Management* 11, no. 4, pp. 451–464.

Jacobs, A. 2017. *How to Think: A Survival Guide for a World at Odds*. Currency.

Jacoby, O. (Producer), and Rudavsky, O. (Producer). 2011. *Bloomberg Risk Takers: Michael Burry*. Bloomberg.

Janis, I.L. 1972. *Victims of Groupthink: A Psychological Study of Foreign-Policy Decisions and Fiascoes*. Houghton Mifflin Company.

Janis, I.L. 1982. *Groupthink: A Psychological Study of Policy Decisions and Fiascoes*, 2nd ed. Houghton Mifflin Company.

Johnson, S. 2010. *Where Good Ideas Come From: The Natural History of Innovation*. Riverhead.

Kabat-Zinn, J. 1990. *Full Catastrophe Living*. Delacorte Press.

Kahneman, D. 2011. *Thinking, Fast and Slow*. Farrar, Strauss, and Giroux.

Kassing, J.W. 2007. "Going Around the Boss: Exploring the Consequences of Circumvention." *Management Communication Quarterly* 21, no. 1, pp. 55–74

Kegan, R. and L.L. Lahey. 2009. *Immunity to Change: How to Overcome It and Unlock the Potential in Yourself and Your Organization*. Harvard Business School Publishing.

Kelley, T. and D. Kelley. 2013. *Creative Confidence: Unleashing the Creative Potential Within Us All*. Crown Business.

Kelly, L. and C. Medina. 2014. *Rebels at Work: A Handbook for Leading Change From Within*. O'Reilly.

Klaczynski, P.A. and K.L. Lavallee. 2005. "Domain-Specific Identity, Epistemic Regulation, and Intellectual Ability as Predictors of Belief-Based Reasoning: A Dual-Process Perspective." *Journal of Experimental Child Psychology* 92, pp. 1–24.

Knight Ridder Newspapers. February 4, 2004. "Knight Ridder Journalists Honored for Stories on War Planning." www.mcclatchydc.com/news/special-reports/iraq-intelligence/article24470662.html.

Kotter, J.P. 1995. "Leading Change: Why Transformation Efforts Fail." *Harvard Business Review* 73, no. 2, pp. 59–67.

Kotter, J.P. 2012. "Accelerate!" *Harvard Business Review* 90, no. 11, pp. 43–58.

Kotter, J.P. and D.S. Cohen. 2002. *The Heart of Change: Real-life Stories of How People Change Their Organizations*. Harvard Business School Press.

Kounios, J. and M. Beeman. 2014. "The Cognitive Neuroscience of Insight." *Annual Review of Psychology* 65, pp. 71–93.

Kuhn, D., R. Cheney, and M. Weinstock. 2000. "The Development of Epistemological Understanding." *Cognitive Development* 15, pp. 309–328.

Lam, C.F., C. Lee, and Y. Sui. 2019. "Say It as It Is: Consequences of Voice Directness, Voice Politeness, and Voicer Credibility on Voice Endorsement." *Journal of Applied Psychology* 104, no. 5, pp. 642–658.

Landay, J.S. September 6, 2002. "Lack of Hard Evidence of Iraqi Weapons Worries Top U.S. Officials." *Knight Ridder Newspapers*. www.mcclatchydc.com/news/special-reports/iraq-intelligence/article24433348.html.

Lerner, J.S. and P.E. Tetlock. 1999. "Accounting for the Effects of Accountability." *Psychological Bulletin* 125, no. 2, pp. 255–275.

Lewin, K., R. Lippitt, and R.K. White. 1939. "Patterns of Aggressive Behavior in Experimentally Created 'social climates'." *Journal of Social Psychology* 10, pp. 271–299.

Lewis, M. 2010. *The Big Short: Inside the Doomsday Machine*. Norton.

Liang J., C. Farh, and J. Farh. 2012. "Psychological Antecedents of Promotive and Prohibitive Voice: A Two-Wave Examination." *Academy of Management Journal* 55, pp. 71–92.

Litman, J.A. 2008. "Interest and Deprivation Factors of Epistemic Curiosity." *Personality and Individual Differences* 44, pp. 1585–1595.

Loewenstein, G. 1994. "The Psychology of Curiosity: A Review and Reinterpretation." *Psychological Bulletin* 116, no. 1, pp. 75–98.

MacCann, C. and R.D. Roberts. 2008. "New Paradigms for Assessing Emotional Intelligence: Theory and Data." *Emotion* 8, no. 4, pp. 540–551.

March, J.G. 1991. "Exploration and Exploitation in Organizational Learning." *Organization Science* 2, no. 1, pp. 71–87.

Massing, M. February 26, 2004. "Now They Tell Us." *The New York Review of Books*. www.nybooks.com/articles/2004/02/26/now-they-tell-us/.

McFarlin, D.B. and P.D. Sweeney. 1996. "Does Having a Say Matter Only if You Get Your Way? Instrumental and Value-Expressive Effects of Employee Voice." *Basic and Applied Social Psychology* 18, no. 3, pp. 289–303.

McIntyre, L. 2019. *The Scientific Attitude: Defending Science from Denial, Fraud, and Pseudoscience*. MIT Press.

Miller, W.R. and S. Rollnick. 2012. *Motivational Interviewing: Helping People Change*, 3rd ed. Guilford Press.

Miller, W.R. and T.B. Moyers. 2017. "Motivational Interviewing and the Clinical Science of Carl Rogers." *Journal of Consulting and Clinical Psychology* 85, no. 8, pp. 757–766.

Moyers, B. April 25, 2007. Buying the War [Transcript]. *Bill Moyers Journal*. www.pbs.org/moyers/journal/btw/transcript1.html.

Mueller, T. 2019. *Crisis of Conscience: Whistleblowing in an Age of Fraud*. Riverhead Books.

Nadella, S., G. Shaw, and J.T. Nichols. 2017. *Hit Refresh: The Quest to Rediscover Microsoft's Soul and Imagine a Better Future for Everyone*. HarperCollins.

Nemeth, C.J. 2018. *In Defense of Troublemakers: The Power of Dissent in Life and Business*. Basic Books.

Nguyen, S. November–December 2014. "Making Organizations Moral." *Harvard Magazine*. www.harvardmagazine.com/2014/11/making-organizations-moral.

Nyhan, B. and J. Reifler. 2010. "When Corrections Fail: The Persistence of Political Misperceptions." *Political Behavior* 32, pp. 303–330.

O'Keefe, D.J. 2016. *Persuasion: Theory and Research*, 3rd ed. Sage Publications.

Oreg, S. and Y. Berson. 2019. "Leaders' Impact on Organizational Change: Bridging Theoretical and Methodological Chasms." *Academy of Management Annals* 13, no. 1, pp. 272–307.

Park, W.-W. 2000. "A Comprehensive Empirical Investigation of the Relationships Among Variables of the Groupthink Model." *Journal of Organizational Behavior* 21, pp. 873–887.

Pauling, L. 1990. "Interview With Nancy Touchette for The First Molecular Biologist." *Journal of NIH Research* 2, pp. 59–64.

Pickel, K.L. 1995. "Inducing Jurors to Disregard Inadmissible Evidence: A Legal Explanation Does Not Help." *Law and Human Behavior* 19, pp. 407–424.

Pinker, S. 2018. *Enlightenment Now: The Case for Reason, Science, Humanism, and Progress*. Viking.

Pinker, S., M.A. Nowak, and J.J. Lee. 2008. "The Logic of Indirect Speech." *Proceedings of the National Academy of Sciences* 105, no. 3, pp. 833–838.

Quinn, A. and B.R. Schlenker. 2002. "Can Accountability Produce Independence? Goals as Determinants of the Impact of Accountability on Conformity." *Personality and Social Psychology Bulletin* 28, no. 4, pp. 472–483.

Rogers, E.M. 2003. *Diffusion of Innovations*, 5th ed. Free Press.

Rohan, M.J. 2000. "A Rose by Any Name? The Values Construct." *Personality and Social Psychology Review* 4, no. 3, pp. 255–277.

Rosenberg, M. 1965. *Society and the Adolescent Self-Image*. Princeton University Press.

Sanchez, C. and D. Dunning. 2018. "Overconfidence Among Beginners: Is a Little Learning a Dangerous Thing?" *Journal of Personality and Social Psychology* 114, no. 1, pp. 10–28.

Satterstrom, P., M. Kerrissey, and J. DiBenigno. 2021. "The Voice Cultivation Process: How Team Members Can Help Upward Voice Live on to Implementation." *Administrative Science Quarterly* 66, no. 2, pp. 380–425.

Schein, E.H. 2017. *Organizational Culture and Leadership*, 5th ed. Wiley.

Schroeder, J., M. Kardas, and N. Epley. 2017. "The Humanizing Voice: Speech Reveals, and Text Conceals, a More Thoughtful Mind in the Midst of Disagreement." *Psychological Science*, 28, no. 12, pp. 1745–1762.

Schwartz, S.H., J. Cieciuch, M. Vecchione, E. Davidov, R. Fischer, C. Beierlein, A. Ramos, M. Verkasalo, J.-E. Lönnqvist, K. Demirutku, O. Dirilen-Gumus, and M. Konty. 2012. "Refining the Theory of Basic Individual Values." *Journal of Personality and Social Psychology* 103, no. 4, pp. 663–688.

Schwenk, C.R. 1990. "Effects of Devil's Advocacy and Dialectical Inquiry on Decision Making: A Meta-Analysis." *Organizational Behavior and Human Decision Processes* 47, pp. 161–176.

Seery, M.D., S. Gabriel, S.P. Lupien, and M. Shimuzu. 2016. "Alone Against the Group: A Unanimously Disagreeing Group Leads to Conformity, but Cardiovascular Threat Depends on One's Goals." *Psychophysiology* 53, pp. 1263–1271.

Sheldon, K.M. 2004. "Integrity [Authenticity, Honesty]." In *Character Strengths and Virtues*, eds. C. Peterson and M.E.P. Seligman, pp. 249–271. Oxford University Press.

Simonton, D.K. 1995. "Foresight in Insight? A Darwinian Answer." In *The Nature of Insight*, eds. R.J. Sternberg and J.E. Davidson, pp. 465–494. MIT Press.

Simonton, D.K. 2011. "Creativity and Discovery as Blind Variation: Campbell's (1960) BVSR Model After the Half-Century Mark." *Review of General Psychology* 15, no. 2, pp. 158–174.

Sitkin, S.B. 1992. "Learning Through Failure: The Strategy of Small Losses." *Research in Organizational Behavior* 14, pp. 231–266.

Smerek, R.E. 2017. *Organizational Learning and Performance: The Science and Practice of Building a Learning Culture*. Oxford University Press.

Stanovich, K.E. 2008. "Higher-Order Preferences and the Master Rationality Motive." *Thinking & Reasoning* 14, no. 1, pp. 111–127.

Stanovich, K.E. and R.F. West. 1997. "Reasoning Independently of Prior Belief and Individual Differences in Actively Open-Minded Thinking." *Journal of Educational Psychology* 89, no. 2, pp. 342–357.

Stanovich, K.E., R.F. West, and M.E. Toplak. 2016. *The Rationality Quotient: Toward a Test of Rational Thinking*. MIT Press.

Staw, B.M., L.E. Sandelands, and J.E. Dutton. 1981. "Threat Rigidity Effects in Organizational Behavior: A Multilevel Analysis." *Administrative Science Quarterly* 26, no. 4, pp. 501–524.

Stouten, J., D.M. Rousseau, and D. De Cremer. 2018. "Successful Organizational Change: Integrating the Management Practice and Scholarly Literatures." *Academy of Management Annals* 12, no. 2, pp. 752–788.

Sunstein, C.R. and R. Hastie. 2015. *Wiser: Getting Beyond Groupthink to Make Groups Smarter*. Harvard Business School Publishing.

Tetlock, P.E. and D. Gardner. 2015. *Superforecasting: The Art and Science of Prediction*. Crown Publishers.

Thaler, R.H. 1987. "Anomalies: The January Effect." *Journal of Economic Perspectives* 1, no. 1, pp. 197–201.

Thaler, R.H. 2015a. *Misbehaving: The History of Behavioral Economics*. Norton.

Thaler, R.H. 2015b. "Richard Thaler With Malcolm Gladwell on Misbehaving." www.youtube.com/watch?v=4-dkZOz9nQw.

Thaler, R.H. 2017. "Richard H. Thaler—Biographical." NobelPrize.org. www.nobelprize.org/prizes/economic-sciences/2017/thaler/biographical/.

Thaler, R.H. and S. Benartzi. 2004. "Save More Tomorrow™: Using Behavioral Economics to Increase Employee Saving." *Journal of Political Economy*, 112, no. S1, pp. S164–S187.

Thompson, L.L. 2003. "Improving the Creativity of Work Groups." *Academy of Management Executive* 17, no. 1, pp. 96–109.

Tiku, N. August 13, 2019. "Three Years of Misery Inside Google, the Happiest Company in Tech." *Wired*. www.wired.com/story/inside-google-three-years-misery-happiest-company-tech/.

The *Times* and Iraq, ed. May 26, 2004. *The New York Times*. www.nytimes.com/2004/05/26/world/from-the-editors-the-times-and-iraq.html.

Torres, T. 2021. *Continuous Discovery Habits: Discover Products That Create Customer Value and Business Value*. Product Talk, LLC.

Tsai, M-H. and C. Bendersky. 2016. "The Pursuit of Information Sharing: Expressing Task Conflicts as Debates vs. Disagreements Increases Perceived Receptivity to Dissenting Opinions in Groups." *Organization Science* 27, no. 1, pp. 141–156.

Tyler, T.R., K.A. Rasinski, and N. Spodick. 1985. "Influence of Voice on Satisfaction with Leaders: Exploring the Meaning of Process Control." *Journal of Personality and Social Psychology* 48, no. 1, pp. 72–81.

Tyler, T.R., P. Degoey, and H. Smith. 1996. "Understanding Why the Justice of Group Procedures Matters: A Test of the Psychological Dynamics of the Group-Value Model." *Journal of Personality and Social Psychology* 70, no. 5, pp. 913–930.

Vadera, A.K., M.G. Pratt, and P. Mishra. 2013. "Constructive Deviance in Organizations: Integrating and Moving Forward." *Journal of Management* 39, no. 5, pp. 1221–1276.

Van de Ven, A.H. and A.L. Delbecq. 1971. "Nominal Versus Interacting Group Processes for Committee Decision-Making Effectiveness." *Academy of Management Journal* 14, no. 2, pp. 203–212.

Von Stumm, S., B. Hell, and T. Chamorro-Premuzic. 2011. "The Hungry Mind: Intellectual Curiosity is the Third Pillar of Academic Performance." *Perspectives on Psychological Science* 6, no. 6, pp. 574–588.

Warren, D.E. 2003. "Constructive and Destructive Deviance in Organizations." *Academy of Management Review* 28, no. 4, pp. 622–632.

Watkins, S. 2015. "Lessons From the Collapse of Enron and the Complexity of Whistleblowing." University of North Carolina. https://youtu.be/RSMnvCMS0W8.

Weick, K.E. 1984. "Small Wins: Redefining the Scale of Social Problems." *American Psychologist* 39, no. 1, pp. 40–49.

Weick, K.E. 1989. "Theory Construction as Disciplined Imagination." *Academy of Management Review* 14, no. 4, pp. 516–531.

Weick, K.E. 1995. *Sensemaking in Organizations*. Sage.

Weick, K.E. and R.E. Quinn. 1999. "Organizational Change and Development." *Annual Review of Psychology* 50, pp. 361–386.

Weick, K. E. and K.M. Sutcliffe. 2007. *Managing the Unexpected: Resilient Performance in an Age of Uncertainty*, 2nd ed. Wiley.

Weingart, L.R., K.J. Behfar, C. Bendersky, G. Todorova, and K.A. Jehn. 2015. "The Directness and Oppositional Intensity of Conflict Expression." *Academy of Management Review* 40, no. 2, pp. 235–262.

Welsh, D.T., L.D. Ordóñez, D.G. Snyder, and M.S. Christian. 2015. "The Slippery Slope: How Small Ethical Transgressions Pave the Way for Larger Future Transgressions." *Journal of Applied Psychology* 100, no. 1, pp. 114–127.

Wemple, E. March 19, 2013. "The Media's Iraq War Failure." *The Washington Post*. www.washingtonpost.com/blogs/erik-wemple/wp/2013/03/19/the-medias-iraq-war-failure/.

Westphal, J.D. and M.K. Bednar. 2005. "Pluralistic Ignorance in Corporate Boards and Firms' Strategic Persistence in Response to Low Firm Performance." *Administrative Science Quarterly* 50, pp. 262–298.

White, R.K. and R. Lippitt. 1960. *Autocracy and Democracy: An Experimental Inquiry*. Harper Brothers.

Willingham, D.T. 2007. "Critical Thinking: Why is It So Hard to Teach?" *American Educator* 31, pp. 8–19.

Wolf, S. and D.A. Montgomery. 1977. "Effects of Inadmissible Evidence and Level of Judicial Admonishment to Disregard on the Judgments of Mock Jurors." *Journal of Applied Social Psychology* 7, pp. 205–219.

Yan, T.T., S. Tangirala, A.K. Vadera, and S. Ekkirala. 2022. "How Employees Learn to Speak Up from Their Leaders: Gender Congruity Effects in the Development of Voice Self-Efficacy." *Journal of Applied Psychology* 107, no. 4, pp. 650–667.

Zeelenberg, M. 1999. "The Use of Crying Over Spilled Milk: A Note on the Rationality and Functionality of Regret." *Philosophical Psychology* 12, no. 2, pp. 325–340.

About the Author

Ryan E. Smerek is an associate professor and associate director in the Master's in Learning and Organizational Change program at Northwestern University. He is the author of *Organizational Learning and Performance: The Science and Practice of Building a Learning Culture.* Over the last 20 years, in addition to organizational learning, Ryan has taught, researched, and published on the learning process of new executives, how culture impacts performance, and how to lead change and innovation. He publishes a blog titled *Learning at Work* on *Psychology Today*. He received a BA from Dartmouth College, an EdM from Harvard University, and a PhD from the University of Michigan.

Index

Alignment
    vs. conformity, 113
    defined, 112
    forms of, 113
    independent thinking, 112, 113
American Actuarial Association, 47
Antecedents of eminence, 30
Anticipating regret, 133
Appreciative Inquiry, 75–78
Autocratic and democratic leadership
    styles
    alignment, 112, 113
    conceptual distinction, 107
    conflict-abundant organization,
      112
    independent thinking, 108
    management principles, 105
    power distance orientation, 114
    social climates, 106
    studying effects, 106
    value-expressive, 110
Autocratic behavior, 109, 112
Autocratic leadership, 106, 107, 111
Avoid groupthink
    blunt disagreement, 118
    communicate the expectation
      for independent thinking,
      119–120
    company advocate, 125–126
    debates rather than disagreement,
      126–127
    direct solicitation, 126
    evaluate ideas on merits, 122–124
    open-mindedness, 117
    pluralistic ignorance, 116
    promote accountability, 120–122
    social psychology, 116
    stating your position, 117
    structured ideation process, 124

Behavioral economics, 32, 34
"Big 5" accounting firm, 35

Capital campaign, 11, 12
Career limiting maneuver (CLM),
    83–84
Change management, 49–51, 87,
    89, 91
Cognitive entrenchment, 29, 30
Command-and-control environment,
    49
Conformity *vs.* alignment, 113
Constructive deviance, 46–51, 68
Credibility and framing issues,
    78–81
Critical thinking, 21, 23–31, 35
Critical trials, 7
Culture and change management, 50
Curiosity, 1, 21, 31–35

Debt financing and tuition, 12
Decision-making process, 5, 107
Defensiveness, 59, 61, 65, 85, 86,
    118, 135
Demonstrate your core values, 57
Deviant anger, 54
Diffusion of Innovations, 88, 99
Digital transformation, 87, 89, 90
Direct *vs.* indirect challenges, 64
Dog collars, 51
Dual threshold model, 53

Effective communication, 86, 89
Effective idea selection, 27–29
Emotional regulation, 53–58
Enron-like behavior, 37
Ephemeral conversations, 70
Ethicists, 138
Expressed anger, 53

Face-to-face conversation, 70
Fact-value distinction, 15–18
Fair audience, 110, 111, 113
Formal authority, 21, 53, 81, 83, 85,
    96, 124

Groupthink, 21, 105, 115–117, 119, 126, 128
Guided mastery, 140–142

Hypernorms, 47, 49, 51

Idea variation, selection, and evolution, 27
Impropriety threshold, 53, 54, 56, 58, 81
Independent thinking
    alignment, 112
    avenues and opportunities, 3
    benefits of, 19
    consumer trends, 1
    decision-making process, 5
    defense of the company, 2
    defined, 4
    deliberation, 19
    enthusiasm, 2
    experience of, 3
    free of willful distortions, 3
    model of, 18–21
    ongoing feedback, 4
    performance evaluation process, 4, 5
    time and investment, 28
Internal efficacy, 143
Investment community, 30

January Effect, 34

Knight Ridder, 43–46

Leadership styles, 21, 105–115
Leading change
    asking forgiveness, rather than permission, 91–96
    change tactics, 89, 90
    digital transformation team, 90
    mental barriers associated, 102
    phases of change, 97–103
    speaking up and then implementing change, 83–91
    types of changes, 89, 90
Learning Through Failure: The Strategy of Small Losses, 101

Means efficacy, 143, 144
Misbehaving: The History of Behavioral Economics, 34

Mortgage-backed security, 24–26
Motivational interviewing, 68

Performance evaluation process, 4, 5
Persuade without authority
    asking questions vs. being direct, 59–65
    assumed positive intent, 80
    benefits and drawbacks, 71
    in conversation, 71
    credibility and framing issues, 78–81
    message medium, 69–71
    presenting evidence, 66–69
    procedural considerations in speaking up, 71–74
    sleeper effect, 79
    using social proof, 74–78
    in writing, 70, 71
Persuasive message, 54
Planned change, 97–99, 102
Plausible deniability, 61, 70
Pluralistic ignorance, 116, 117
Power distance orientation, 114, 115
Procedural justice, 98, 110, 111
Professional integrity, 21, 46–52
Prohibitive voice, 18
Promotive voice, 18
Protected value of "truth," 42, 43
Psychological reactance, 86, 90
Purposeful obfuscation, 133

Really backtrack, 85
Regretting inaction, 129–139

Save More Tomorrow, 32
The Science of Successful Organizational Change, 87
Self-efficacy
    guided mastery, 140, 141
    induce a conversation, 141
    internal efficacy, 143
    means efficacy, 143
    participants, 141
    psychological safety, 143
    research on, 140
    social learning, 142
    sources of, 142
    verbal persuasion, 142
    vicarious learning, 142

Side-pocketing, 25
Situational Test of Emotion
        Management, 58
Sleeper effect, 79
Slippery slope, 137
Slow hunches, 31–35
Sobering experience, 67
Social proof, 23, 74–78, 81, 88, 100,
        143
Soft advocacy approach, 63–64
Speaking Up, 1, 14, 19, 21, 36, 41,
        42, 47–51, 53–59, 65, 71–74,
        83–91, 105, 113, 114, 124,
        133–135, 139–142
    implement change, 83–91
    procedural considerations, 71–74
Structured ideation process, 124, 127
The Structure of Scientific Revolutions,
        34

Toxic culture, 51
T-shaped experiences, 30, 31

Value-based argument, 16
Values
    definition of, 15, 16
    reason and truth, 40–46
    subjectivist stance, 16
    trans-situational goals, 15
    value-laden, 16
Verbal persuasion, 142
*Victims of Groupthink: A Psychological
        Study of Foreign-Policy
        Decisions and Fiascos*, 115
Viewing implementation, 101
Vocalizing dissent, 13
Voice cultivation, 79
Voice directness, 61
Voicer credibility, 61
Vulnerability of looking stupid,
        35–40

Weapons of mass destruction
        (WMDs), 43, 44
Where Good Ideas Come From, 31